THE POWER OF THE ZIP

*Reinventing the Way You Talk
One Conversation at a Time*

D0168153

JILL KAMP MELTON

Acknowledgments

This book has been brewing in my psyche and my teaching for almost forty years.

First, I would like to thank all those people who have ever spoken lovingly to me. You have been a real encouragement. Second, I would like to thank all those people who have spoken abusively to me. You inspired me to pursue, relentlessly, another way.

I have always known deep inside that some ways of communicating help and some hurt. I am glad to help you readers in your search for another way. Maybe I can save you some time and some pain.

To my husband, thank you for loving me unconditionally. You have provided a safe place for me to grow.

To my children, thank you for giving me stories to tell.

To my friends, thank you for bearing with me through the ups and downs.

To my students, more than seven thousand, thank you for letting me try out my theories on you. You have been very cooperative.

To Sylvia Shaffer, thank you for your patience and your first edits. They were invaluable.

To my parents, who always wanted me to be on stage, I hope it's okay that I traded the stage for the written word. I might get a wider audience and writing helps me process my thoughts and experiences.

To my teachers, I am not sorry I drove you crazy with my questions. You helped me achieve more than I might have without your challenges.

To you, dear readers, thanks for being curious. Together we can do more than we can do alone.

Table of Contents

CHAPTER I

The Power of Perspectives

When it comes to communicating effectively, most people are caught in a dilemma. On the one hand they lament, like Bart Simpson, the TV cartoon everyman, "I don't know! I don't know why I did it, I don't know why I enjoyed it, and I don't know why I'll do it again!" On the other hand, if you are a person who wants to achieve some self-knowledge and maturity when you are talking, thinking about talking, preparing to talk, and reflecting on how you just said what you said, you don't want Bart to be your role model.

This book is written for all people, leaders in the workplace, at home, and with friends who want and need integrity and maturity to guide what they say and do.

Most books designed to help you communicate will give you sample strategies and dialogues to use when talking with others.

That's in this book, but there is more.

This book is different.

I am including several self-assessments and worksheets that will help you replace what you used to do with what you can do using **The Power of the Zip and thirty-four** other powers.

I have studied how we use language for more than forty years. Bart Simpson and the rest of us, the solution to our dilemma is at hand!

The Six Topics of Conversation

It seems to me that there are six possible subjects of conversation that people can focus on:

1. Things	4. People
2. Events	5. Ideas
3. Places	6. Feelings

What do you like to talk about the most? In the assessment that follows, list six people you speak with most frequently. Then assess which subject from the above six you like to talk about most. When you are finished, ask each person on your list what they like to talk about the most, without showing them your list. This will indicate if your favorite subjects match theirs or miss the mark. This can be an easy way to deepen your relationships: speak with others about the subjects they like the best.

This can also help you decode why some of your conversations are not fulfilling. For example, if you like to talk about ideas and you often converse with someone who likes to talk about things, you now have an explanation as to why you are often bored. Likewise, if you like to talk about events and someone you like to speak with prefers to talk about people, one of you or both of you will be bored and avoid conversing.

People I speak with most frequently	Things	Events	Places	People	Ideas	Feelings
1.						
2.						
3.						
4.						
5.						
6.						

Nine Ways We Use Language

I have long thought about how we use words, and I have ranked the styles from the highest form to the least desirable. The ways we use words help to determine whether or not we are heard, paid attention to, and ultimately have an impact.

> 1. There is **professional and/or thoughtful, reasoned conversation:** What would leaders and managers, clergy, parents, friends, and elected officials be able to accomplish if this was the primary type of conversation people used? What would it be like if we could expect others to use language this way?

A modern novelist, Stephanie Barron, who writes in the style of Jane Austen, invented a female character who refers to a potential suitor, evaluating him principally on the way he uses language. "He is very elegant, to be sure, but I could not be entirely easy in his company, Aunt. He lacks...conversation."[1] That resonates with me because I have heard many men and women lament the fact that they went on a date with someone, "and I couldn't talk to them." They might as well be echoing Ms. Barron's sentiment that someone lacked conversation.

When we say someone lacks conversation, I think we really mean that they lack professional and/or thoughtful, reasoned conversation. Reasoned conversation is a skill that can be learned if you are motivated. I mentored two young teenagers, at their parents' request, because they wanted to be accepted by and attend a prestigious private high school in their area. Determining that they "lacked conversation" and the kind of thoughts that would make meaningful answers to the questions on the school's challenging application and interview process, I showed them the movie *Gandhi*, starring Ben Kingsley. More than three hours long, it held these young people spellbound and provided us with hours of conversation. When we finished this conversational tutorial, they were ready to answer thought-provoking essay questions in print and during the face-to-face interview. Both teens were accepted by the school and they excelled in their studies.

Key Question to consider:

How often do you think you use reasoned and thoughtful conversation?

> **2. Debate** is a formal type of reasoned conversation and can also be a scholarly sport or competition. Debate is formally thought of as the presentation style heard in Congress or a state legislative body, at public political forums, especially used during election seasons, and in school clubs that still have an extra-curricular activity called "debate."

Debate is also the style of communication that is favored in think-tank organizations and in corporations that want to maintain or achieve their superiority in cutting-edge technology, like Apple, Google, Facebook, Microsoft, and others. It is favored because decades of studies seem to show that debate encourages the imagination to soar and creativity to exceed known limits.

How do you want others to see you? Do you want to be seen as someone who is easy to be with or as someone who challenges almost everything others say?

People who challenge your thoughts instead of pondering them are debaters. Unless you have signed up for the sport of debate, you may feel victimized by debaters.

Formal debates have trained referees who try to assure that both sides are in compliance with the rules. Informal debates have no referees and so one or both parties may find that their emotions are unfairly played upon.

Using words to manipulate other people and play on their emotions can be perceived as a power struggle. One person tries to win all the points, assert his or her power to do so, and the winner is like the victor in a boxing match who stands with fist in the air, asserting dominance.

If someone you like is not easy to talk to, it may reflect that they are baiting you to debate, which is not what you want to do. It's best to establish some norms with this person to avoid a style of conversation you don't like.

On the other hand, the effect of debate on creativity has been measured and findings seem to indicate "that debate and criticism do not inhibit ideas but, rather, stimulate them....debate may be less pleasant, but it will always be more productive." [2]

Key Question to Consider:

Do you engage in debate when you speak?

> **3. Banter** is a quick, back-and-forth exchange of words, not as formal as debate. Banter is almost a sport that values one-upmanship. This is a learned skill and is the only way people talk in some cultures, like in the large urban areas of New York City and Chicago. A newcomer to these settings might not even know what is being talked about if banter is the style of conversation that predominates. Buzz words, slick phrases, humor, and some coarse language are used. Some people are raised with the notion that speaking is banter, like volleyball. I toss out some words, you volley back, back and forth, until the person who says the most words with skill wins.

I hear two types of banter. One is "high-level" banter, an intellectual exercise between two people who are challenging themselves to use intellect and humor to develop a thought and entertain one another in the process. With the goal to use language succinctly, stimulatingly, and innovatively, the end product of this kind of banter is intellectually fulfilling and feeds on itself. As it grows, sometimes the people who are bantering exceed even their expectations of how witty and funny they can be. Professional actors do this in "improvisation," a technique made popular in the TV show "Whose Line Is It Anyway?"

The second type of banter is low-level and is characterized by street talk, words that are slang or the kind of words that are usually banned in polite workplaces. It is the kind of talk that helps people feel regular, normal, and comfortable in bars or other places where people let their hair down and don't worry about embarrassing one another. Instead of using fists, the people who banter this way seem to find it intellectually stimulating in a coarse way. Those with delicate ears, like me, better get out of the way or the finely tuned barbs will hit and sting.

Unless you are a gifted comedian with a genius for devising the perfect quip, you will fail at banter and you will feel bad about it in the process. As with professional actors who excel in improvisation, this is a skill that can be learned but you have to be quick, smart, agile, and energetic to keep up until a winner is declared. If you are tired after conversing in a quick back and forth, you have probably been bantering. How much of your day is occupied with this type of conversation?

When someone is quick to use sharp, biting wit, that habit is also a form of banter. Banter with other people can easily be a lose-lose sport. Some workplaces thrive on banter and sarcasm. It is not uncommon for people in these places to have high blood pressure, weigh more than they want to, and have many health issues.

What do we miss if our main style of communicating is banter? James Joyce, Irish author and deep thinker, pinpoints it for me: "Language is ambiguities probing ambiguities." Yet we think we can listen and understand right off the bat! How cheeky we can be!

If you think of conversation as banter, you might feel compelled to get the "last word." That is a signal of serious competitiveness, which can create noise pollution and poison relationships.

Key Question to Consider:

Do you almost always want the last word?

> **4. Idle chatter/water cooler talk/chit-chat/small-talk** include the typical topics of weather, sports, hobbies, the latest electronic gadgets, current fads, and movies. People like to engage in idle chatter to take a break from periods of heavy concentration

There is a valuable purpose for small talk when used consciously. A proactive, positive use of small talk is when you use it in order to put other people at ease. If you are a host at an event where there are attendees who don't know one another, small talk can relax others and help them feel welcome and not the center of attention. I usually start with, "Where are you from?" That question can keep us talking for quite a while and is a useful tool that opens the door for an authentic relationship that could develop over time. Conversation at this level can encourage engagement, not boredom.

Idle chatter can also be fun for some, but not for those who like to talk mostly about ideas.

Key Questions to Consider:

Do you look for every excuse to interrupt what you are doing to find someone to engage in small talk? What are the benefits you get from engaging in small talk?

> **5. Idle gossip or planned gossip** is filled with "he said, she said" and tidbits of information about other people. "Did you hear about this one dating that one?" "I heard that he was asked to leave before he was fired."

What's wrong with gossip? It depends. Facebook now keeps gossips busy. It's easy to find out what other people are doing. Just access their page and you will know who just had coffee, who's washing their car, whose relatives are visiting, and who is going shopping. It's easy to know what music people like and all the flotsam and jetsam of people's lives is on display if you care or if you are just nosy. Some people live for the tidbits of others' lives. I guess if they don't hurt anyone with the information, it's okay. As for me, I once wrote in a journal, "If I'd only shut up, I'd have a book."

Planned gossip borders on slander, which can land you in a lawsuit that you may not have intended. Besides the money you will need to defend yourself, you, as the slanderer, are guilty of using verbal violence and there is no place at home or with friends for violence against another person.

Key Questions to Consider:

Have your friends or family ever overheard you gossiping? When you talk, are you often looking around to see if someone can hear you? If you were overheard, would that make you uncomfortable? If you have answered yes, you may be gossiping, perhaps even more than you intend.

> **6. Whining and complaining** are different levels of the same effort. Whining is less intense. Complaining is more aggressive. Both are contagious at home and with friends and can become ingrained habits in the culture.

Some friendships are based on these activities. Without complaining and whining, you sometimes feel that there is nothing left to talk about.

At work, do you initiate or join others who enjoy whining and complaining? They whine or complain about the way it used to be, the way it is now, the way it's going to be, the lack of resources, the misuse of resources, the boss, the employees, and every other thing that exists at work.

When your kids whine at home, how do you feel? If you socialize with co-workers, neighbors, family, basically anyone, does the conversation degenerate into whining?

If you are honest with yourself, do you think you contributed to the habit of whining? Have you somehow given the impression that it's okay?

Key Question to consider:

Do you know people with whom you engage in complaining as your main sport?

> **7. Teasing,** it seems to me, is a form of bullying because teasers usually pick on someone who is less skilled in banter than they are. Defenseless people being teased can't keep up. The teaser sees that the other person appears wounded and that gives the teaser a momentary thrill and an elusive sense of power.

There is always a winner and a loser here and if someone is repeatedly the loser, that person becomes very insecure and sometimes paralyzed, unable to achieve what is required at work or at home. This is what teasing does; it hurts. Sometimes the scars last forever. It is not true that "sticks and stones may break your bones but words will never harm you." That's the deep wish of someone who has been victimized by words: to avoid injury. This person wants and needs some protection.

Most of us know that "things are often NOT what they appear to be." So why do we get blind-sided by the very thing we know is out there to get us?

Because we are human.

When people declare to others that they have nothing more to learn, I don't think they really mean it. They are just afraid that they may not be able to change. They may have been teased into paralysis.

When people tell us that they are trapped in circumstances that are beyond their ability to change, don't believe them. They just don't know how. They might not believe they have any effectiveness at all. They are being bullied and teased by their own fears or by real bullies that wield undue power.

However, we can change ourselves, our reactions to bullies, and our own fears. Millions of people have become adults with the scars of youthful teasing forever etched in their psyches. It takes conscious effort to break free from the patterns of thought that hold us hostage. So instead of the old taunt, it's important to remember, **"Sticks and stones may break my bones, and words can break my spirit."**

I have seen people who have been so beaten down by teasing that they have chronic stomach problems and their very posture is stooped. They look wounded and behave wounded.

Look at people under the age of eighteen. If you see distorted posture, crestfallen looks, and people who have stomach problems, you may be looking at people who have been teased and perhaps verbally abused in their young lives.

Key Questions to Consider:

When you think you are "just" teasing, have you ever received feedback that you have hurt someone's feelings? Was it verbal or displayed in body language? Have you ever teased someone to tears? If so, you are probably causing harm.

> 8. Robust language, aka coarse, salty language or cursing, can be a habit for some and uncomfortable for others to hear. But salty language and cursing has no place at home or with friends, in my opinion, unless you just hit your finger with a hammer and blood is pouring out!

I find it fascinating that the Latin definition of cursing or profanity refers to that which is "in front of" or "outside the temple," referring to items not belonging to the church. Over time, this meaning changed to the current meaning, language that is insulting, rude, vulgar, desecrating, or showing disrespect.

My research into profanity led me to hundreds of quotes from people who think this kind of language enriches the nation. Obviously, I am counter-culture in my views about language. Verbal abuse and nastiness disguised as cultural richness seems like a cop out to me. **Maturity takes work. Lack of maturity**

may be easier and more fun. In the long run, however, it can cost you your job, your relationships, and fulfillment.

  9. Verbal abuse is another form of violence. Abuse in any form hurts others.

If we are to treat others as we want them to treat us, we should have a zero tolerance for it. Unfortunately, many people experience verbal abuse as part of their childhood and think there is no way out. Either everyone in their world indulged in verbal abuse, or it was so every day that they were numbed by it. Then, when they try to create a fairer and more reasonable world in their adult lives, they don't know how.

I am aware that if you think verbal abuse is okay, just fun, and "the way I talk," you may not continue reading. As I share my thoughts, I feel like a diet counselor who is telling you to give up eating meat and chocolate. I have seen speakers talk about those subjects and duck to get out of the way of objects being thrown at them.

I will duck and keep sharing.

Who are the abusers? They could be anyone: a teacher, parent, sibling, other relative, sports coach, librarian, bartender, scouts leader, store clerk, co-worker or any classmate.

Civility can be learned. If anyone has ever accused you of using verbally abusive language, you might want to have a professional counselor help you evaluate the situation.

It helps if you try to understand the mind and character of an abuser. **Isaac Asimov said, "Violence is the last refuge of the incompetent."** When someone is insecure and feels helpless and powerless to change his or her own life, let alone the lives of others, they often resort to violence. Psychologists teach that anger is a secondary emotion. That means you get angry at others to avoid feeling your own deep hurts. It seems easier to put them off on someone else than to deal with them on your own.

What would psychiatrists and psychologists do for a living if all cases of verbal abuse stopped, if all people were convicted that words are not weapons? They could work proactively, teaching people about healthy ways of interacting.

Nelson Mandela once said, "For to be free is not merely to cast off one's chains, but to live in a way that respects and enhances the freedom of others."

Verbal abuse respects no one. Being free must include the freedom to choose your words carefully.

There are examples of twisted marriage etiquette that run amok on night-time TV and movie screens worldwide. Rude, crude, and abusive relationships sell tickets and advertising. They also make divorce lawyers rich and rob us of our peace. **Don't let anyone rob you of your peace and joy.**

Now is the time to give up these bad habits and learn new ways of relating and communicating with others.

Key Questions to Consider:

Have you ever, whether premeditated or in a fit of anger, been abusive to someone else? What happened? What did you say or do?

Communication Style Self-Assessment

What styles do you use? What styles are the most appropriate to use? How do you answer these questions? How do the people you interact with answer these questions?

Use this chart of communication styles to fill in the names of the people you communicate with most. Then put a check on the dominant style of communication you use with them. If you dare, give them a copy of this chart and ask them to assess what style or styles they think you use with them.

Name of Person	Reasoned Conversation	Debate	Banter	Chit-Chat	Whin-ing	Gossip	Teasing	Robust	Abusive

Key Questions to Consider:

What did you learn from this assessment? How did you rate yourself? How did others rate you? If there were surprises both in your self-ratings and the ratings others gave you, how can you account for the gap between what you thought and what others thought?

Sometimes we give messages to others that we don't intend, either messages that make us seem more open, intelligent, and caring than we are, or the opposite. Asking the people who assessed you some open questions will help you get more information about the kind of communicator you are. Paying more attention to what you say and how you say it will help you improve or maintain your effectiveness.

Take this into the workplace and ask your employees, peers, and boss how they would assess your communication style. Is there anything they notice that damages your effectiveness, maintains it, or improves it?

You might want to ask a teenager, "You rated me as someone who talks a lot, maybe in the idle chatter column. Tell me more. I'd like to know what you hear when I speak."

Or you might want to ask a friend, "You rated me as someone who banters a lot. Tell me more. Do you think it is a barrier to an intimate, honest friendship between us? Tell me what you think."

If there are relationships you have with some others that need to be reinvented, take heart. First, start with this assessment and do your part. Then, give a copy to other people, one at a time.

Once you discover how you are perceived by others, you can begin to look more objectively at how you communicate. Even if the perception by others is not at all what you intend, you can begin now to self-assess and recalibrate, renewed with their eyes, to see what might be misleading them.

Think of the cameras in luxury cars that can project a 360-degree view of what's all around the vehicle when you begin to back up, park, or move into areas where you have blind spots. The vehicle is engineered to make a noise to keep you within safe boundaries. People have blind spots, too, and we need to thoughtfully look into them, one at a time, to learn more about ourselves and how others see and hear us.

There was a time several years ago when I realized I needed to improve my communication style with my three sons. I wrote about my awareness in a letter and gave it to them. I wanted them to know that I was more teachable than it may have appeared. One of my sons still has the letter.

It is never too late to rethink how you communicate with others. Even if you are in "relationship jail" and your close friends and family don't want to have anything to do with you, you can begin again. Start with a salesperson, mail deliverer, or co-worker, anyone.

The most important thing is your motivation.

Key questions to consider:

Will becoming mature and responsible in the way you use language get you a promotion and a raise? Will it save your marriage? Will it save your job? Will it improve your self-esteem? Could it improve your health?

If you answered yes to any of these questions, keep reading.

CHAPTER 2
The Power of Caring

"So what, who cares, what does this have to do with me?"

If you want to be heard when you speak, you first need to address the concerns of your listeners, who are asking themselves, "So what, who cares, what does it have to do with me?

How will you know what someone cares about, thinks about, complains about, and is worried about? In advance of the conversation, the talk, or any presentation you will make, ask questions, listen when others talk, and look for clues.

Then address those concerns first to show that you know what is uppermost in their minds.

Before I made a presentation to a group of coast guard admirals in the 1990s, my research revealed that oil spills were a big concern for them. I referenced that concern first before I got into my subject matter and consequently I had their attention because I had earned credibility. They felt I knew them and that meant my remarks were not "one size fits all." They would be customized for the coast guard.

Another presentation I made for the American Association for the Advancement of Science was designed to help a large group of post-doctoral scientists network with colleagues outside of their membership. In a conference call before the event, I clearly became aware that they didn't like networking. They felt that they should be respected and sought after on the basis of their degrees, their research, and their contributions to the world of science. So I had to teach them something they didn't want to learn. They had no idea how my topic would be of help to them.

I changed the title of my presentation from "Networking" to "Networking: The Art of Authentic Relationships." Why was that necessary? These brilliant men and women erroneously thought that the only way to network was to use one another, like opportunists out for personal gain. I was able to bridge from their mindset to mine, appealing to their desire for authenticity more than for networking.

I have discovered that if you establish an authentic relationship with a colleague, you will automatically want to help them and they will want to return the favor. So helping someone else first creates that authentic relationship where networking and sharing are the way you behave. Aha! Finally I had shown them why getting to know other scientists, collecting business cards, and schmoozing at receptions would help them grow and expand their areas of influence within the scientific community. **Give first.**

If I hadn't addressed their questions, "So what, who cares, what does this have to do with me?" the entire audience would have tuned me out.

A middle manager I have taught describes how her caring for employees sets the tone for her management style.

"I absolutely love people. This I am sure of. All shapes, sizes, ages, types. When I go into a facility, I make a point of getting some one-on-one time with each employee. I don't set up a meeting. I just find them when they are alone in the break room or on a computer or wherever. I try to feel them out, connect with them, ask about their family, kids, hobbies, life, and then really listen to what they are saying and what they are not saying. I think employee satisfaction, motivation, and drive come from employees feeling valued. I try to ensure that my employees know that I value their ideas and opinions and respond to them. I believe in them. I feel that the vast majority of employees come to work and try to do a good job. I make sure my employees know that I will fight to the end to defend them when they have tried to do the right thing. I also let them know that I will hold them accountable when they don't follow rules or regulations.

"Wherever I work there are at least one or two 'difficult' employees. I try to look for the spark of spirit in each of them. Who knows what hardship, trials, or experiences have led them to be the way that they are? I have found that after you hold one or two of them accountable in a private discussion, they seem to get the word out better than I can that everyone is being held to certain standards. They may give me a tough time about doing that, but I think it lets everyone else in the facility know that I care about the health of the team as a whole."

For me, this person is the managerial role model for the Power of Caring.

Another manager describes the Power of Caring as "believing in" her employees. This is in stark contrast to the "beat'em up" method of using power and force.

"Some of my employees get beat up pretty good in training. So besides teaching them technical skills, I try to let them know that I believe in them.

Not just by words, but by my actions. I can't think exactly of what I do, but I stay very casual and relaxed. If I need to over-ride them to fix something immediately, I don't make a huge deal about it. During the debrief, I ask them what the thought process was that led to his or her action. Then we discuss it and the other, better options. **I have had a lot more success with this than with others who have the beat'em up' method of managing.** I don't see any reason to belittle anyone. I address the improper decision, but don't attack the person."

Because I believe that any thoughtful, reasoned conversation is "a presentation," **a presentation occurs any time you are talking to at least one other person.** That person could be a co-worker, a boss, an employee, a spouse, a child, a friend, neighbor, pastor, literally anyone. The implication of this definition means that **we make presentations all day long. You may not consider yourself a public speaker, but you are.**

It must be common knowledge by now that the *Book of Lists* has a list of people's top fears, and the fear of public speaking ranks higher than the fear of death. A colleague, Tom Zahler, humorously quips that therefore most people would rather be in the coffin than delivering the eulogy.

I conclude that most people use language poorly and interact poorly because they fear public speaking. We talk a lot and so we are bad at doing the very thing we do all the time.

How can we overcome this fear and relate to others with confidence and caring? Let's do some assessing.

How often do you notice that others tune you out? Do you often see yawns when you speak, people consulting their iPhones or Blackberries or other electronic devices? How can you figure out what they need to hear so that the next time you speak you will be heard?

Unless you have someone's attention, you have no chance of being heard. Seeing them stop in their tracks, tilt their heads, and have the mask of attention on their faces is not enough. You need to arrest their minds.

How do you do that? You need to say something that is unexpected and that addresses some topic you are pretty sure they care about.

How do you do that?

When I teach this to groups, I declare at the beginning, **"Just because you said something doesn't mean it was heard."**

"...some neurologists now say that **the basic human need is to be the 'sparkle in someone's eye.'** ...Life makes sense and is empowered by joy when people are in relationship with those who love them and are sincerely 'glad to be with them.'" [1]

If you are a manager, you might bristle at having to stroke the egos of the people who work for you. Parents may balk at thinking they have to let their kids know that they are "the sparkle in their eye" all the time. If you are not the emotional sort, you may think that this child is too old for that sort of display. Friends, spouses, and many others may also tire of giving affirmation as much as it seems to be required. **Actually, no one is ever too old to be told that they are special, appreciated, and loved.**

Remember, it's not about us; it's about the other person.

If you have the desire to communicate effectively with at least one other person, you need to communicate to your listener that you care. This validates the person and when others are affirmed, when they feel that you care, you are maximizing the chance that your messages will be heard.

When you speak to anyone, if you don't care, whether or not you say anything about caring for the other person, he or she knows it. How? It's something we sense, and we can sense it within twenty seconds of talking with someone. It's more than a feeling; it's the total presence of the other person.

When I was in my twenties and an acting student, my teacher, actress Olympia Dukakis, asked the whole class, "What characters do you really want to play in your careers as actors?"

I was stunned by my own response. My answer to myself was, "No one." I was too busy figuring out how to "play" me, how to be me for real; playing other parts was not my ambition. Then what was I doing in professional acting school? Answering that question propelled me to change majors, finish graduate school in one more year, not two, and get on with my life.

Why didn't I want to play other characters? I began to realize that I didn't really like a lot of other people. I had no trust, no interest, no deep concern for others.

Nine years of psychotherapy and a decision to put God in the center of my life changed that. Now, more than forty years later, I have a love for others that pops out of me. I have learned to be caring and, in turn, others, family, and friends seem to care for me

Key Questions to Consider:

Do you really care for others? A small circle of others or a whole big ocean of others? What gets in the way of your being able to care for others? Who could help you overcome this obstacle?

Neutralize the Whiners

Another Power of Caring is that you will have the potential to **neutralize the whiners.**

Do you have friends, a spouse, or children who whine a lot?

I have been blogging about the process of writing this book and a reader responded to the topic of whining: "Thanks for your blog on whining...it was very timely. The whole family has been ill for nearly a week and there has been lots of whining. Me included! But your blog adjusted my perspective!"

My blog presented six perspectives to deal with whining:

1. Whining can be positive. It dilutes the potential violence that could happen when people don't vent and then resort to passive-aggressive silence. Whining, venting, and complaining are far better than exploding. Whining may even better than weeping in the corner with self-pity.

2. Whining can also be a barometer of morale in the workplace or at home. It gives you information about what people are feeling. If they are not getting enough positive attention, people may whine because they mistakenly feel that negative attention is better than no attention.

3. Some family and work cultures have a "habit of whining" built into them. The whiners don't think there is anything abnormal about their yakkety-yak. They are just trying to fit in.

4. If any of these examples ring true for you, how about instigating a new habit, like "**Mean Mondays**"? On Mondays, you can set a boundary with anyone in your sphere of influence. It's okay with you if they complain. Then it may be easier to institute "**Positive Tuesdays**." On Tuesdays, the same people can only say what is good, uplifting, positive, and encouraging. Customize the rest of the week as you need to.

5. Eventually, you can transition to asking this question on Mondays, "Is there something you want to talk about to change the way we interact, and relate with one another? What are those things? Let's talk about them." In this way you can "mine for the nugget," asking open questions until you hit the mother lode of information that was there all along. You just never got that deep or that direct. Now may be the

time. Like the video on YouTube with people playing basketball and someone in a gorilla suit walking between them from one side of the court to the other, people, when asked to describe what they see, often just talk about the players. Few see the gorilla. It's as big as a real one would be and yet they miss it. What are you missing that you need to see and deal with? Whining may give you good clues.

6. Sometimes whiners will not give up their sport. They are too selfish, or jealous, or angry, or their whining may just be a symptom of a serious flaw in the system of how you do business or relate. If that is true, you may need a third, neutral party, a facilitator who can help get to a deeper level and direct you to the solution.

When the cartoon anti-hero of pop culture, Homer Simpson, said, "Kids, just because I don't care doesn't mean I'm not listening," he was the caricature of the listener who hears but does not care and doesn't understand how damaging the lack of caring can be.

It's not because I don't have a sense of humor that I'm not laughing at "The Simpsons." I feel pierced to my heart of hearts just thinking about how Homer might reflect American culture. Workplaces that are run by people who don't care become mean-spirited centers where people are wounded daily. The workplace becomes a triage center without medical personnel and many workers are the walking dead. In the same way, kids who are raised by non-caring adults are damaged and it can take years for the damage to be rooted out and repaired.

Potential Landmines of Caring

People who do not excel in caring for others may fear that showing their feelings will impair their credibility and their authority. Perhaps the quote, "They don't care what you know until they know that you care" should be tattooed on our hearts. It doesn't matter if the quote originated with basketball coaching legend John Wooden or with John Maxwell, the leadership author, coach, and mentor. In my opinion, it's motivating and true. If you are seen as caring, it doesn't follow that you will be seen as weak or a wimp. Nothing is more motivating than experiencing the empathy of a caring person and having him or her shed a tear with you or commiserate with you on the latest bit of difficulty in your life. Without words, a caring person can convey that he or she "feels your pain."

CHAPTER 3

The Power of the Present

Key Question to Consider:

What is the most important minute of your day? Many people say, "My first cup of coffee," "seeing my baby smile," "when I get home from work and sit and talk with _____," or "whenever I have some quiet time." It took me forty-four years to learn the answer and I wish I had known it earlier.

"The most important minute of the day is the minute you are in."

I have seen pictures of a clock that has the word "Now" twelve times instead of numbers all the way around. If that were your clock, how would it change the way you spend your minutes.

What are the other implications? Some people go through their days as though some particular minutes, conversations, or actions were more important than others. They do themselves, others, and their work a disservice. It means that if you have an important meeting at 3:00 pm, the meeting is not what you should be "saving yourself for."

When my children were small and I worked part time, I was torn when they misbehaved or created stress. "Don't they know I have to do _____ later today? I can't use all my energy now. I have to save some for later." How wrong I was.

How would your life change if it were true that the most important minute of your day was the one you were in? How would you change the way you interacted with others? How would you change what you do in your day when no one was looking?

Being present means that you are fully engaged in what you are doing when you are doing it. Your mind, emotions, body, breathing, spirit, all of you is there with nothing dangling elsewhere.

Think of a ballerina who makes precision turns. In each micro-second of each part of each turn, her focus must be "There, there, there, and there." If she forgets that discipline even for a split second, she would get impossibly dizzy and fall.

Think of someone with a bow and arrow and a target in his/her sights that must be hit. The shooter must focus mind, body coordination, breathing, and will all toward the bull's-eye on the target. There must be nothing else in the world more important than that target.

Once, when I shared this idea in a class, a thoughtful participant spoke to me afterwards. He proposed that I take this concept one step further. He said, "If what you say is true, then **the most important minute of your day is the most important minute in someone else's day."**

Profound and true.

So our minutes impact the minutes of others. We should not squander any.

Potential Landmine of Living in the Present

When you begin to live your life as though the most important minute of your day is the one you are in, others may think you are intense. As long as it doesn't prevent someone else from relaxing and being less intense than you, I regard intensity as an asset.

There is an icon on my phone, from the application I have downloaded called emoji that has a picture of a tent with an eye inside. When I text that icon to a close friend, she knows that I am feeling "intense." Having a sense of humor about one's intensity can help you lighten up for a good laugh. It can also help those you interact with.

CHAPTER 4

The Power of the Zip

The **Power of the Zip** is the "magic" that happens when you speak with someone else and you keep quiet for as long as it takes for the other person to contribute. The Power of **the Zip** allows other people to unfold to themselves first and gives them permission to think in front of you, and it doesn't matter who speaks first. It creates a safe environment where people can share without penalty; you will seem more trustworthy in the process.

The **Zip** unleashes the power of "wait." Helping you calm down, **the Zip** gives you time for your thoughts and feelings to catch up with the speed of events happening around you. It gives you the opportunity to find out more about other people and adds to your credibility because listening makes you seem wise.

For me, the most important part of the **Zip** is that it awakens your sense of curiosity about others and the way things might work. A colleague of mine says, "I wonder what they'll come up with that I don't know about." An active mind and a sincere interest in learning keep us on the edge of new things until the day we die. Without this sense of curiosity and wonder, we are the walking dead.

The power of the **Zip** means that you will not talk when someone else is talking, no matter what. Short of a fire or other serious emergency, you will not talk, even though words are swirling around inside your brain and you think you will explode in volumes if you keep quiet for one more minute.

Key Question to Consider:

When is talking considered noise pollution? When it is uninvited. To me, the sound of thinking is one of the most beautiful sounds in the world.

Potential Landmines of the Zip

I think one reason people don't use the **Zip** more often is because it slows you down and takes time. That's the very reason we need to use it. **We speak in haste and repent in leisure and regret it for the rest of our lives.**

The **Zip** can also cost us feelings. By this I mean it is more likely that we will get involved and have empathy for those in situations that may be messy. So emotions overcome us whether or not we have invited them, and we may be distracted by these emotions when we try to listen well. Habits and mannerisms such as grinding your teeth, working your jaw, and fidgeting betray us. Incidentally, paying attention to these muscular responses to emotion may save you expensive dentist bills. Take note, however, that these habits can become serious barriers in what could otherwise be a useful exchange.

When allowing the **Zip** to punctuate your communication style, you will learn things and be challenged to think differently and act differently. In fact, you may have to change course, and change is uncomfortable for many.

That's the irony, that people need to be agile and resilient to change and yet change is the very thing we may fear most, even more than public speaking.

A colleague challenged me to think about the times when it is okay to "unzip." That is, when is it okay to speak and not worry about what you say? Here's the checklist:

- When something you need to share is true AND
- When it is necessary to share it AND
- When it is the right time to share it AND
- When you truly feel that what you plan to say will add real value.

The right time is not only when you have the time. It is important to discern when the other person is ready to hear what you have to say. Blurting and speaking in haste violate the sensitivities I am asking you to cultivate in this book.

CHAPTER 5

The Power of Silence

How much noise is there around you? Do you work with background music or "talk radio" or do you prefer the stillness of silence?

When you are with another person, does someone always talk? Do you ever just exist together, not doing anything, not thinking, just being together in time and space?

I enjoy this kind of communication with my grandchildren sometimes. I think we bond this way. We are comfortable with silence and just are together.

I also enjoy silence with my husband. It sometimes allows us to communicate on a much deeper level than we would with words.

Silence is not necessarily the absence of thought, ideas, and feelings. Silence can be as powerful as light.

Key Questions to Consider:

Is silence a friend or foe for you?

My husband and I have watched the movie *Into Great Silence*, a documentary about monks in France who have pledged their lives and their ministry to a vow of silence.

Netflix describes it this way:

"Director Philip Gröning's study of the Grande Chartreuse monastery introduces a world of austere beauty as it follows the daily activities of the resident monks, whose silence is broken only by prayer and song. With no sound save the natural rhythms of age-old routines, the documentary, a Special Jury Prize winner at the 2006 Sundance Film Festival, captures the simplicity and profundity of lives lived with absolute purpose and presence."

Almost three hours long, this movie had both of us fascinated. My husband quipped reverently that the lifestyle of cloistered monks was the ultimate **"Power of the Zip"**!

I wondered and still wonder how long I would last, living a life unbroken by a verbal sharing of ideas with others. The Carthusian monks in the film have written and published many books and perhaps that communication outlet would meet the need to talk and share with others. I don't know.

I do know that I write, think, and study better in silence. My husband likes music, smooth jazz, classical, pop, and easy listening. I like those also, but not when I am writing, thinking, and studying. Hence, we have divided the house into zones. When I am writing, he respectfully listens to his music in the bedroom/man cave/study or on the back porch.

How do you deal with silence? How much silence is enough for you? Can you have the silence you require in the workplace? Think-tanks might be able to have rules of silence but people who work in the public sector and have to be accountable to customers and stakeholders every day may not be able to establish quiet zones.

What about at home? If your home is filled with people who make lots of noise and you prefer silence, how do you cope?

A friend and insightful consultant from Kenya, Dr. Nyaki Adeya-Weya, told me, "Do not say anything before you are sure your word is worth more than your silence." She doesn't know whom to credit with the quote but she remembers hearing a wise Indian old man say it in "A Love Story," a Brazilian Emmy-winning television soap opera produced by Rede Globo.

When listening to other people as they take time to express themselves in words, body language, pauses, and expressiveness, how often do you wait in expectation of what they will say? Too often we think we know what they will say and prepare our responses before we even hear what they are about.

When listening to anyone, focus totally on "this present moment," and wonder what the other person will say. In this way you will be open to learn something new, hear in a new way, and receive a message that you might have otherwise missed. **Since people sometimes say things without saying things, linger in the silence for a while.**

The biggest Zip of all is the Zip of the spirit. In silence there is an opportunity for you to ponder and reframe your thoughts, your words, your mental models, your hopes, your dreams, your heart, and your very soul.

Potential Landmines of Practicing Silence with People

Unless you live in a monastery where the vow of silence is agreed upon as a good thing, silence all day at home or at work, when you are in a position of authority and responsibility, could have perils.

I have some friends that wear serious noise-canceling headphones when concentrating. Useful if used wisely, these could be dangerous as a parenting technique because you might miss emergencies and lose the ability to hear your children at play and at work and your neglect could have serious consequences.

Have you heard the expression that "silence means consent"? The perception that this is true is the chief reason silence has perils as well as powers. Verbal silence must be broken at some point to prevent people from misinterpreting your actions and making assumptions that are wrong.

Another landmine is that some people fake open listening and the speaker doesn't know it. So you talk on and on thinking you have been heard, when in fact you have been artfully tuned out. Unless you pause and risk silence when you speak, you may never know if you were tuned out or not.

If someone talks to you and you disagree with this person's perspectives and opinions, your silence may be misinterpreted as agreement. If you wimp out and choose not to speak about the areas you do not have in common, you may find yourself in a phantom relationship with someone else. They think you are a friend and that you like to hear them talk. In fact, you do not agree with most of what this person says.

Phantom relationships can be dangerous because if you let them persist for weeks, months, and perhaps years, when you finally have the courage to confront the situation, the pain for the other person may be shocking. If you are guilty of this deception, get some training in Crucial Confrontations so that the conversation will have a chance of being successful.

CHAPTER 6

The Power of Wait

The power of wait is closely connected to the power of **the Zip**. It controls time in that you must wait for someone's mind to get into gear before they speak. What do you do while waiting? You continue to be calm and patient, and watch the other person's ideas hatch. How long does it take for a bird to break out of an egg, a flower to unfold in spring, a butterfly to come out of a cocoon? It depends. Just wait.

In conversation, some people are comfortable waiting. My second son had this ability when he was young. When he was growing up, I found myself talking more with him because he listened. Waiting comes naturally to him and consequently people seek him out to confide in him and share their deepest thoughts and feelings. My oldest son has cultivated it in adulthood

Waiting also gives the people you are talking with the gift of time, time to rearrange themselves.

When someone begins to believe that you will wait for this rearrangement to occur, your credibility as a caring listener strengthens. If you are perceived as sincere and the real deal, people will begin to take whatever time is necessary for ideas to formulate when they speak with you.

Waiting, with the expectation that some good will come out of the wait time, is powerful because it is calm. People usually think better when not pressured to respond immediately.

Waiting in this positive way gives the wait time its power. While waiting for brain synapses to connect and align and realign, the person who has been asked a powerful question feels accepted, respected, and valued. That's when people are at their best.

Waiting also helps us remove the garbage and clutter from our minds by winnowing the essential from the unnecessary. Our minds are filled with preconceptions, assumptions, and quick guesses as to what others think, not to mention what we think. Waiting helps us delete the junk and helps us get to the essence of a thought with fewer detours. When we give other people permission to wait until they have clear thoughts, we enable the process to become leaner. (Working with managers who train in Six Sigma ® methods to attack inefficiencies in business processes, I have come to appreciate the benefits of "lean" in conversation.) [1]

We limit our minds and erect barriers where they may not be necessary. We are afraid to face the thoughts that come to us when we wait. It never hurts to ask for the moon if the moon is really what you want. It's not about whether or not you get the moon. It's about facing the truth that you want it.

Even if you can't get the moon, the power of wait may help you figure out that you really do want the moon and why you want it. You may never have allowed yourself to think that impossible thought before. A former leadership student who used to work as a bush pilot in Alaska, and therefore was someone who, in my opinion, used to do impossible things daily for twenty-five years, once gave me a greeting card of appreciation that quoted the Queen of Hearts from *Alice in Wonderland* saying, "Sometimes I believe in as many as six impossible things before breakfast."

Key Questions to Consider:

So where do you stand on the scale of waiting to think of and believe in impossible things: once a year, once in a lifetime, or once a day? If your answer is not at all, let's have a talk. Do you have time? Can you wait awhile to consider this?

If you always believe only in "possible" things, you may never move to another level of thought, belief or action about those things or perhaps many other things. You may need to cultivate the ability to wait.

How should you begin to believe impossible things? Banish the heckler inside you. The heckler is the voice that calls you stupid, a dreamer, lazy, ineffectual, or any other epithet that is unlovely. You have given this heckler squatter's rights inside your head and heart. Evict the beast now! That beast may be a compilation of every thoughtless word that has ever been said against you by others and it doesn't belong in you.

Now invite only positive influences inside. Be careful what you read, watch, and think about. Be your own bouncer and don't let the negative crowd in.

After evicting the heckler, lean back and allow yourself to listen to the air, the birds, the weather, every little bit that surrounds you. Listen to the inside of you. And pretty soon you will begin to awaken to thoughts of impossible things. Your heart will pound and you will become more awake than you have been in a long time, perhaps ever.

The power of wait gives you time to banish the heckler and to soar.

The power of wait also protects people from rushing.

Waiting is both calm and powerful because you give power to the time in between silence and talking when you might otherwise "make something happen." Waiting means that there is a chance for factors other than your overactive problem-solving efforts to intervene on your behalf.

Waiting helps remove the garbage, the clutter from your mind. We get lockjaw of the mind, the thinking gear gets stuck, and waiting gives us a chance to lubricate our thinking so that new ideas can flow.

Waiting winnows the unnecessary from the essential.

It helps you figure out what you want.

It helps you figure out what you feel.

It helps you figure out what other people want.

It helps you figure out what other people feel.

It is healthy: it lowers blood pressure and reduces stress.

Another Key Question to Consider:

Why do people have trouble waiting?

Some people can't zip it. They literally don't have the ability to. They might have attention-deficit disorder, be a compulsive talker, or believe the bumper sticker that says, "He who says the most words wins." This person may know a lot and feel it criminal to withhold information. He or she might have a passion to share passionately. This person might have the strength of "Woo" and be gifted in talking, marketing, and sales. [2]

Talkers could talk all day, just stop for dinner, and continue talking all night. A talker might not be able to get to sleep at night without rehashing the day or other conversations regardless of the time. This can cause hardship for his or her close friends or family.

A talker might be an extrovert, or woefully need attention, work as an auctioneer, or find it's just plain too hard to shut up.

Perhaps some people talk all the time because they are intensely lonely or are desperately seeking for someone to love them. In this case, we often want to run away because we may not have the desire or ability to meet their needs and help replace their loneliness with caring.

The three self-assessments below will help you find out more about yourself and your conversational strengths and weaknesses.

Self-Assessments

I. Make some copies of this assessment. Fill one out and ask a few people to also fill it out about you.

My Strengths in Conversation	My Weaknesses in Conversation
1	1
2	2
3	3
4	4
5	5
6	6
7	7
8	8
9	9
10	10

II. I like to talk with the following people:
1.
2.
3.
4.
5.

III. This is what I like about those conversations:
1.
2.
3.
4.
5.

IV. I don't like to talk with the following people:
1.
2.
3.
4.
5.

V. This is what I think gets in the way:

1.

2.

3.

4.

5.

Put a check in the box that most clearly characterizes what you do. Only check one answer for each statement.

Characteristic	Always	Sometimes	Never	Don't Know
1. I talk too much				
2. I talk too little				
3. I think before I talk				
4. I am impulsive (blurt out)				
5. I talk when I'm angry				
6. I talk when I'm hungry				
7. I talk when I'm tired				
8. I talk when I'm lonely				
9. I talk without facts				
10. I talk with facts				
11. I listen before talking				
12. I can remember conversations				
13. People seek me out to talk with me				
14. What I say is memorable				
15. When upset, I talk to the Lord first, not people				

Rating Scale

If you have checked "sometimes" or "always" for at least four of numbers 3, 10, 11, 12, 13, 14, and 15, you have demonstrated the ability to **Zip It** when it counts.

If you checked "sometimes" or "always" for at least four of numbers 1, 2, 4, 5, 6, 7, 8, and 9, you need to re-evaluate your communication style. You may be using numbers 4–9 of the ways we use language (The Power of Perspectives) too much. That behavior will bring about consequences you may not intend. Go back, look at that chapter, and rethink what you say, how you say it, and what your goal is when you talk.

The perceived power that others have over us exerts real pressure on us. If we think other people are waiting for us to say something, whether or not that is true, we will talk to fill the silence. **Peer pressure is real. Imagined peer pressure is also real.** Remove the "shoulds" from your life about the way you think other people want you to interact and react in conversation and you may find a "real you" that you have never explored or rarely used. It certainly will prevent others from taking you for granted. They will have to stop and listen to you in new ways because they can't predict your words anymore.

Do you have the habit of worry? Some people do and that is a powerful force that keeps them talking and talking in an attempt to alleviate their anxieties. People who have the habit of worry are likely to hate this habit and so they do things to try to tamp it down. They may smoke, drink, or indulge in other addictions in an attempt to self-medicate. It doesn't work. The root of why they worry will haunt them until they get to the bottom of it. This requires work, just like digging out the roots of an old tree. But unless you do get to the bottom of it, it will get in the way of mature thinking, behaving, and speaking. **Isn't that the goal of a person who wants to excel: to be mature in thought, actions, and speech?**

Some people won't Zip it; they lack the motivation to try. Egocentric, always right, and incapable of delegating, they may be mean-spirited, possessed, feel victimized, or need to be good at something and talking is IT. Or it's just too hard to stop.

What is the benchmark as to how many words are enough? "Be not tedious in discourse, make not many digressions, nor repeat often the same manner of discourse." That's what George Washington said. [3]

The title of the 1970s British musical *Stop the World, I Want to Get Off!* highlights the central problem of waiting. The treadmill of the lives most of us lead is running fast. We may want to get off, but we don't know how. Until we learn how to drop out of the rat race and reduce stress in our lives, we find that waiting is hard to do. When we fill the "wait" with activities that we think will get us where we want to go, we may miss the anticipation and excitement of just waiting to see what will unfold.

If you close your eyes and imagine that you are in a boat going down a river, you can almost feel the current of the water taking it in one direction. Imagine that feeling. You don't have to do much except sit tight and wait. Now imagine that you get tired of waiting and you take up a paddle that was lying at your feet and start to paddle. You are striving and your trip is now different. The first way, you allow events to unfold. The second way, you make something happen.

In communications, there is a time and place for both actions, the waiting and the striving to make something happen. Which do you do most often? If you use the paddle more than the "wait," you will miss a lot.

If you don't have clarity as to what you want, then it will be hard to really hear what other people want.

Become known as the person who tolerates thinking about seemingly impossible things. I guarantee the quality of your relationships will soar and so will the morale of others.

I worked with a gifted facilitator who was born and raised in Missouri and she liked to tell the story of the cow paddies. You see, in Missouri, in the fields, the cows leave little remembrances called cow paddies everywhere. As she told the class, "You need to dodge the cow paddies to walk through the fields and not get hit," she energetically dodged and jumped and ducked in the classroom to make her point. (I enjoy copying her in my classrooms because I love the exercise and people think it's fun to watch me running and bobbing around.)

What's my point? Angry, discontented people who crave attention, even negative attention, will hurl cow paddies of words everywhere. If you let yourself get hit, you will get drawn into their negativity. If you duck, you escape the hit and perhaps may get the hurler to quit this behavior. When other people are negative, they don't like to be negative in a vacuum. If the words don't stick, eventually the sport loses its appeal and the negative person may stop that behavior. It's worth the chance to test this. Ducking successfully is another technique if you want to use the power of wait. If you are not a target, the person may have to **Zip it** and walk away.

It's no fun to argue alone.

Waiting, in between asking powerful questions and getting the answers, also helps you clarify what you want. You know you want things to change. You may not know what that exactly looks like or how you will get it. Waiting helps you sort through your own thoughts and to try on other ideas for size.

Even more insightful, **waiting helps you figure out what you feel**. Sometimes we are completely frustrated when we don't get what we want and we barely know what words to use to describe the feelings. How many times have you been nonplussed, stymied, and completely out to sea about how you feel about some problem that has come up in a relationship? You know something is wrong, but

35

the words and the feelings are too intertwined and need to be disentangled, like a mass of old wire, before you can act with a clear head.

Waiting also helps you figure out how others feel.

Communications practitioner, John Powell, SJ, wrote about this extensively in three books. [4] I read them in the 1970s and have reread them again recently because his perspectives helped me learn about myself and communication. The emotional checklist he devised is useful to us with others when you are in the throes of complicated feelings you don't understand. If it surprises you that the menu is so long and that many feelings can be so complicated, perhaps this is a section you should ponder.

This chart has been adapted from his Checklist of Emotions in *The Secret of Staying in Love*, pp. 156–159. [5]

When you are overcome by emotion but are at a loss to figure out what emotions are swirling around inside you, use this list to try to make sense of your feelings. You can't figure out what others feel until you know what you feel. They go hand in hand. Countless marriages have dissolved because frustrated partners can't figure out their own feelings, let alone the feelings of the other. No doubt organizations have failed because of misread feelings. When people are clueless, they make poor decisions and that erodes confidence and morale.

Accepted	Accepting	Affectionate	Afraid
Alarmed	Alienated from others	Alienated from self	Angry
Anxious	Anxious to please others	Apathetic	Appreciated
Attractive	Awkward	Beaten	Handsome
Bewildered	Brave	Calm	Cheated
Closed	Comfortable	Committed	Compassionate
Competent	Concerned for others	Confident	Confused
Connected	Contented	Like a Cop-out	Cowardly
Creative	Cruel	Curious	Cut off from others
Defeated	Dejected	Dependent	Depressed
Deprived	Deserving punishment	Desperate	Disappointed in myself
Disappointed with others	Dominated	Domineering	Eager to impress others
Eager to please others	Easily manipulated	Easygoing	Embarrassed
Envious	Escape, desirous to	Evasive	Evil person, like an

Excited	Exhilarated	Failure, like a	Fatalistic
Fearful	Feminine	Flirtatious	Friendless
Friendly	Cold	Frustrated	Generous
Genuine	Giddy	Grateful	Gratified by personal accomplishment
Grudge-bearing	Guilty	Gutless	Happy
Scorned	Hateful	Homicidal	Furious
Hopeful	Hopeless	Hostile	Humorous
Hurt	Hurt by criticism	Hyperactive	Hypochondriachial
Hypocritical	Ignored	Immobilized	Impatient
Inadequate	Incompetent	Inconsistent	In control
Indecisive	Independent	Inferior	Inhibited
Insanity, afraid of	Insecure	Insincere	Involved
Isolated	Jealous	Judgmental	lonely

Like a loser	Lovable	Loved	Loving
Loyal	Manipulated	Masculine	Masked
Masochistic	Melancholy	Misunderstood	Needy
Old beyond years	Optimistic	Out of contact with reality	Out of control
Over-controlled	Overlooked	Oversexed	Paranoid
Passionate	Peaceful	Persecuted	Pessimistic
Phony	Played out	Pleased with others	Pleased with self
Possessive	Moody	Preoccupied	Prejudiced
Pressured	Protective of others	Proud of others	Proud of self
Quiet	Rejected	Religious	Remorseful
Repelled by others	Repulsive	Restrained	Rewarded
Sad	Sadistic	Secure	Seductive
Self-complacent	Self-pity, deserving of	Self-reliant	Abnormal

Shallow	Shy	Silly	Sincere
Sinful	Sluggish	Soft	Sorry for self
Stubborn	Stupid	Suicidal	Sunshiny
Superior to others	Supported	Suspicious of others	Sympathetic
Tender	Terrified	Threatened	Tolerant

Torn	Touchy	Triumphant	Two-faced
Ugly	Unable to communicate	Unappreciated	Uncertain of others
Uncertain of self	Understanding	Dull	Unresponsive
Unrestrained	Uptight	Used by others	Useless
Victimized	Vindictive	Violent	Weary of living
Weepy	Winner, like a	Wishy-washy	Wimpy
Youthful	Zesty		

Finally, waiting helps lower your blood pressure and reduces stress, that is, if it is healthy waiting. I coached a person who had high blood pressure and wanted to qualify for the lowest rate possible when buying long-term care insurance. For twenty-four hours before the mandatory blood pressure test, he rested, slept, listened to classical music, controlled his thought life, ate moderately, and militantly refused to allow anything intrude into his calm and solitude. Instead of the156 over 120, which was his usual high blood pressure, it measured 118 over 80.

There were two important lessons learned here. His elevated blood pressure could be changed without medication using planned life-style adjustments. The changes affected his bottom line because he saved thousands of dollars in premiums over the life of his insurance policy. Thoughts affect feelings, which affect one's health.

Potential Landmines of Wait

If your dominant style of handling conflict is to avoid it, you may think that waiting may simply encourage you to avoid it more and you don't want to be branded an "avoider." Perhaps this is true and perhaps it isn't.

A former pastor and very wise man, Dr. Graham Smith, once taught me that there are three questions to ask yourself before you confront anyone about anything. They are:

- Is it true?
- Is it necessary?
- Is it time?

If you are waiting because the thing you need to talk about is true and necessary but the timing is not right, you are not avoiding the conversation. You are simply waiting for the best time to do it. That's wise, not wimpy.

If other people are hurling their cow paddies at you and you successfully duck so they don't stick, you are actively waiting until the air is clear and there are no visible or invisible arsenals of words that are flying through the air. This is also wise.

If you don't wait and don't duck, you are now competing in the sport of negativity with the negative person and, in that competition, everyone suffers. Everyone needs to be rewarded for positive attitudes as well as positive behavior. This practice can become a serious contribution to the emotional maturity of others.

CHAPTER 7

The Power of Pause

For me, the power of pause is a little different from the power of wait. Wait is what you do when you need someone else to play their part in the conversation. Pause is what you do when you find that you have rambled on and on and you need to regroup and rethink what you are saying.

"Please give me a minute. I need to rethink that answer. Perhaps I spoke too quickly. Do you have time to pause, or should I wait a bit for a better time?"

Pause is also what you do when you speak slowly, allowing others to hear your brain crank into gear. When you pause as you speak, you are also giving others permission to do it when they speak with you.

Others learn how to understand their thoughts and feelings as they watch you do it. Don't rush your use of this skill.

Potential Landmines of Pause

When we don't pause, we are in danger of running on, making poor decisions, and not taking the time for our thoughts and feelings to catch up with us.

What I mean by this is demonstrated clearly if you compare old movies with contemporary ones. Since movies try to reflect the culture of their times, the shift in the way movies portray speaking, listening, waiting, and pausing is significant.

The film classic *Roman Holiday* (1953) has reporter Gregory Peck running into a royal princess, Audrey Hepburn. She has gone AWOL to rebel against being controlled. Her desire is to find out what life would be like as a mere commoner. When Audrey and Gregory meet, the first scene is very long, perhaps twenty minutes. The camera allows the actors time for their characters to "take each other in." They look, they think, they feel, they measure one another, and all of this takes time.

Films in the twenty-first century register all this differently. Instead of lots of dialogue, the camera shifts from eyeball to eyeball, smile to smile, facial expression to gestures to carefully controlled emotional details, in mere seconds. The process is sped up since the attention span of Western audiences has shrunk. In 2012, a scene like the one above might last only three minutes.

Commercials exhibit this best, when complicated relationship layers are revealed with a raised eyebrow, a turn of the head, or a slight shrug of shoulders, all in sixty seconds.

In 2006, I helped organize and administer two conferences for reporters in India. Gathering in Bangalore, they were intent on listening to formidable lectures by some brilliant speakers. I was told, "You don't have to schedule too many breaks and the days can be long. The Indians haven't yet been ruined by the media as we have in the US."

It's true. Ever since Marshall McLuhan wrote about the phenomenon that "the media is the message," people can't seem to sit still too long and want information immediately, hence the popularity of texting.

Even medical schools that used to rely solely on long lectures to convey information now have to mix it up with interactive breakout sessions and videos. Professors used to get away with being "data dumpers." Now almost all instruction in any discipline has to be done by "collaborative facilitation." That's why I offer a course called "Transforming from Being a Data Dumper to a Collaborative Facilitator." The version for parents is called "Tune Me Out No More: A Guide for Parents Who Want Their Kids to Listen to Them."

So compared to the long scenes in movies made before 1960, audiences in 2012 want their romance, adventure, science fiction, and mysteries to happen faster.

That's fine in the movie theater. But human beings haven't been rewired to think and feel that fast in reality. That's why I am taking pains here to restore the "wait" and "pause" in normal conversations, especially the important ones that we need to have.

The landmines of the lack of "wait" and the lack of "pause" are shallow interactions. You may miss what you need for understanding, clarity, and mature decision-making.

CHAPTER 8

The Power of Listening

When I was trained as a volunteer counselor for La Leche League, the international organization that helps moms who want to breastfeed their children, active listening training lasted a week. Why in the world would it take that long?

As volunteer counselors, our goal was not to "push" one method of feeding over another. On the contrary, we needed to really hear the heart of the mother, give her confidence in her new role, and even if she chose bottles, help her feel good about her choice. A confident mother was more important than a breast-feeding one. Laying a guilt trip on any mother was the last thing we wanted to do.

We listened, we paraphrased, we asked questions and summarized what we thought we heard, all to make sure we weren't hearing something that wasn't said. We needed to hear the words, the thoughts, the feelings, both spoken and unsaid, in order to be effective. If we were trustworthy, we were more effective, and it was not uncommon for a mother who bottle-fed her first baby to come back for new coaching with a second or third child, to give herself a chance to do it differently.

When we think we are right, when we think we know the way, when we have everyone's best interests at heart, that's when we need to say less, listen better, and Zip it! Otherwise we are not listening openly but are trying to control the conversation.

Listening to "what is" means being open to something that is not the way you want it to be. You do not try to control or change the conversation. To listen, a controller has to replace his or her thoughts and opinions and be open to the thoughts and opinions of others. As Atticus Finch, the fictitious lawyer in the book and movie *To Kill a Mockingbird* by Harper Lee, says, "You never really understand a person until you consider things from his point of view—until you climb into his skin and walk around in it."

Key Question to Consider:

What's required to be a good listener?

- A willingness to suspend oneself and to be in the present with another person
- Curiosity
- Boldness

What gets in the way of open listening?

- Fear
- The old tapes in our mind of past experiences, people, the voices from our past that are hard to silence
- Prejudices
- Assumptions
- Biases
- What other people think
- The limitations of what we know

We must be quiet inside to listen to someone else.

What is it like when we are not heard or listened to? We feel ineffectual, lonely and in need of a do-over.

Here is an assessment to use with others. Ask each person designated on the left side of the table three questions. When you are listening to them, what do they see? What do they sense? What is the result?

Ask them to assess you when they think you are listening effectively and then to assess you again when they think you are not listening effectively. Compare the results.

Assessment for Effective Listening

Person Taking Assessment	What I See	What I Sense	Result
Spouse			
Child #1			
Child #2			
Child #3			
Best Friend			
Peer at Work			
Employee at Work			
Boss			

Assessment for Listening That Needs Improvement

Person Taking Assessment	What I See	What I Sense	Result
Spouse			
Child #1			
Child #2			
Child #3			
Best Friend			
Peer at Work			
Employee at Work			
Boss			

Gather data. Think about it. If you think there is room for improvement, what will you do about it? If this is a time to change some behaviors, would you like someone to hold you accountable for the changes? Who might that be? How frequently will you talk about the changes you are making?

If open listening is not one of your strengths, it might be a result of what the Myers Briggs Type Indicator, MBTI, calls a preference for introversion. This means you might recharge your energy by being alone, rather than being out and about with others.

A very insightful manager I taught put it together this way, "An extrovert has to prepare to listen. An introvert has to prepare to speak."

Key Questions to Consider:

Do people listen to me? When, why, for how long?

If you really care about improving your listening, the conversation you might have with others could begin like this:

"I have noticed that when we talk, I see yawns and fidgeting. Since I value our friendship and I hope you do also, I'd like to know what gets in the way of you listening to me. I want to listen to you in a way that makes you feel heard and valued. Is there anything that I do or say that I may not be aware of? Any feedback you can give me will help."

Potential Landmines of Listening

There is some risk that the person listening to you will think that his listening implies he agrees with or must obey what you say. Listening, as I am using the concept here, means to hear and to respond, not necessarily to agree or obey. If you listen, ask questions, and begin to negotiate your response, you are still listening. If you end up doing something different from what you were requested to do, that doesn't mean you didn't listen. It means you did not agree with the request.

Another landmine is that sometimes we take offense at what is said and that prevents us from listening openly. Here's how it works.

Someone I care about says something to me and strong feelings begin to well up inside. I'm not sure where these feelings are coming from and even how to describe them. I just know that I am emotional and beginning to feel defensive.

I'm thinking, I don't want to pursue this topic and I want these feelings to go away. I am feeling increasingly more hurt and defensive. I need to protect myself. I don't want to go public with this struggle and I want it to stop.

I stiffen up and hope my muscles protect my emotions from bubbling out to expose my pain.

The key is to **paraphrase and redirect**. How can I remember in that moment to do that?

Try this.

Me: "You seem to be pressing in on me to talk about _____. Is that true? Can you tell me more about your interest?"
Me: (Stage direction for me: "Zip it!")
You: "Well, I just want you to talk about _____."
Me: "So you are insisting that I talk about _____. What is your intent?"
Me: (Stage direction for me: "Zip it!")

If you keep re-paraphrasing, at some point the "insister" will reveal to the insistee the hidden agenda.

Most often an insister has a hidden agenda. If they are not up front and open about it, I will feel assaulted by their insistence and you probably will, too.

We need to ask questions to bring the hidden agenda out in the open, otherwise it will hang in the air and we will feel emotional and the unspoken issues loom larger than they might be. The mystery of unspoken issues is that they make the threat of the unknown worse.

Sometimes in the insister's desperation to rattle the insistee, they will frame their remarks in a context that gets bigger and bigger. They go from the detail that concerns them to the whole of your relationship together to your relationship with other people at work and at home.

Stop and rescript your habit of taking offense, becoming emotional and feeling paralyzed. If you feel that the insister has a hidden agenda, ask first, "What is your intent?" Remember to Zip it after you ask that powerful question.

CHAPTER 9

The Power of the Question

What role models do we have if we want to ask questions that inspire others to change their behavior or learn more about themselves?

Historians say that Socrates is the father of the question and his name gave a label to a system of education, the Socratic method, which is based on asking "Socratic questions." He taught his equally famous student Plato using questions rather than giving him answers.

Before Socrates, Biblical scholars credit Hebrew teachers more than four thousand years ago with mastering the art of questioning.

In government agencies and private corporations, managers and CEOs routinely ask their subordinates questions and can transform a working culture in this way:

- How does your work relate to the vision and mission of our organization?
- If you were to add more value to the vision, how would the way you do your work change?
- What can you do differently to meet our customers' expectations and still conform to our vision?

Do you manage in this way?

Likewise, in families, parents who know how to ask open questions can create a positive **mentoring culture**.

Do you parent in this way? Why or why not?

Anyone who has ever seen a TV episode of "Law and Order" knows that lawyers only ask questions to which they already know the answer. Otherwise there would be too many surprises in court and their case would be weakened. I can represent that as:

question + what is already known = interrogation.

The kind of questions I am advocating here are questions to which you don't know the answer. These are the questions that require you to be sincerely curious. The equation for this is:

question + curiosity = ????? or the unknown. If you don't know the answer, the question has the potential to be powerful and valuable.

Key Questions to Consider:

Do you "tell" or do you ask? How would your conversations change with others if you mentored and coached them instead of bossing them?

Why are questions so powerful? An open question asked at the right time to the right person has the power to inspire a person to think creatively, without risk or penalty.

For example, my first boss, Dr. Bertram Joseph, at Queens College in 1969, where I was a full-time instructor in theater, asked me, "What do you want to see your students doing so you will know that they understand what you are teaching them?" He said, "Don't rush. You have a whole year to answer that question."

I took the year and then some and the final answer is in my book *The Actor's Working Process*.[1] The power of Dr. Joseph's question also led me to develop a way of teaching that I still use today. I need to know what I will see students do that shows me they understand and can apply what they have been taught.

How to Do It:

Asking people a key question can help them help themselves. What they learn by doing and thinking will inform their understanding of themselves and their potential for a lifetime of happiness.

For example, here are some questions that anyone might ask during the course of a day:

- What is making you so angry? What led up to this? **(Zip it!)**
- You seem confused. What could you do to fix this? **(Zip it!)**
- What makes it hard to get your work done? **(Zip it!)**
- Exactly what happened? Walk me through it step by step. **(Zip it!)**

Wait for the right time to ask these questions.

It could take many minutes for you to get the answers. If the questions were asked sincerely, and if the person really believed that his or her answers mattered, you would need to sit back, wait, and process the silence. It will be worth the wait. When you respect the thoughts and processes of others, you add to their self-confidence.

If you work in an environment so deadline-driven that there is no time for this type of conversation, you may need a schedule-free zone, a day or week when there are no deadlines and life can find its own pace. If you have never done this, you are about to experience a real breath of fresh air.

Asking a question is a powerful way to arrest the attention of your listener. The power of the well-worded and effectively asked question is dynamite, pun intended. Script your question in advance. Make sure it addresses what your listener needs and wants. When you ask the question, be firm, loud, and clear, and speak slowly enough so that people will get every word. When you are finished, let the words hang in the air. That's the first evidence of **the Power of the Zip**. When the silence hangs in the air and you keep your mouth shut, you are on your way to communicating effectively.

How many of you know that when you talk, other people hang on every word and remember almost all of what you say? I ask this question because it addresses many people's worst fear: that no one listens to them. The inner monologue that goes on sounds like this: "They don't listen and that's why I have to be the boss, act like a boss, and walk and talk like a boss. I don't like it any more than they do but I don't know another way to behave."

When you learn to stop acting like a boss and start acting like a coach and mentor to each person you deal with, you will be heard more. In addition, your employees, friends, spouse, and children will start meeting and exceeding your expectations for creative problem-solving. They may even develop more passion for living.

How does this magically happen? One question at a time. Every time you have a conversation with someone, you have the opportunity to coach and mentor them to exceed their own expectations. I promise you, their expectations for themselves, if they are honest, are far greater than yours.

At age four, one of my granddaughters received a toy that mimicked butterflies coming out of a tube. She and her seven-year-old brother had a net and tried to catch them one at a time. They were enjoying a friendly competition to see who could catch the most. The "butterflies," pieces of fabric shaped like flying insects, were propelled by a motor forcing air up a plastic tube and out into the room.

Suddenly the "butterflies" got caught in the plastic tube and it seemed as if the game were doomed. She cried and was frustrated and a big argument between the two children, as to who caused the problem, threatened to take away their fun.

I simply said, "Let's stop for a minute and look at the process. What makes the butterflies come out of the tube? What gets in the way of this happening? Show me." I waited very patiently as they figured this out. The arguing stopped and they began playing again.

When the game was over, I asked the children to tell me what they learned. I didn't prompt them. They volunteered that the game was disrupted because something was stuck. When they turned their attention to figuring out the problem, they were able to solve it; their tension was gone and they seemed empowered because they had figured something out on their own.

This technique is worth paying attention to. Every time you ask a powerful question that stops another person in their tracks, and gets them to self-reflect and really think deeply about potential answers, you have used a powerful, open question. Make a list of these questions. Share your list with others. See if they are inspired to contribute one or two questions themselves.

Let's compile a starter list of questions here:

• As you look at your work and think about how hard it is to find anything, I am wondering if you can think of some other way that would work better. What ideas come to mind? (Zip it!)
• Is there a way that you might prefer me to interact with you when you don't do what I have expected, a way that I am not using now? (Zip it!) • What ideas come to you when you think about it? (Zip it!)
• What skills and abilities do you have that I don't recognize? (Zip it!) • If you could redesign how you spend your spare time, what would you do? (Zip it!)
• I remember our last argument about _____. Communication broke down and no one was listening to anyone else. In your opinion, what do you think happened to make that fall apart? (Zip it!) • How could we prevent that from happening again? (Zip it!)

• I notice that you are preoccupied today. What's up? (Zip it!)
• You look exhausted and I know you have lots more work to do. How can I support you to get your work done and get some rest, too? (Zip it!)
• I know that you want me to purchase_____. As you are thinking about it, if you could change the way we spend money, what changes would you make? (Zip it!)
• If we had to cut our budget by 10 to 20 percent, what could we do to preserve quality and still save money? (Zip it!)
• Can you tell me anything about how I talk to you that gets in the way of you doing what I ask you to do, or give a specific example? (Zip it!)

These questions use **Zip it!** as a command to obey if you are to be more effective as a communicator. If I were teaching this concept to you face to face, I would say, "**Zip it!**" a few times, and then if I needed to remind you again, I would simply move my fingers across my mouth as though closing a zipper, to make my point. Words would no longer be necessary. In fact some students in my classes repeat the words "**Zip it!**" as I gesture, as if on cue. They get it. I do that because I am trying to help them learn a new habit. If I get them to say "**Zip it!**" enough times, they may internalize it, think it, and actually do it more often. Incidentally, emphasizing the concept helps remind me, too.

Potential Landmines of Asking a Question

Asking questions without caring about the people you are talking with can give others the perception that you are investigating a problem for which they will be held accountable. In conversations that are not investigations, you still may need more information from others and a clear understanding of what other people are feeling in order to make better decisions and handle situations wisely. Take care to ask open questions with no hidden agenda on your part. Otherwise, others will feel interrogated and they will run when you approach with your "questions."

If I am not truly curious about what you have to say, I will prejudge you and your responses and my questions will not open you up or shed new light on the situation we are discussing.

The kind of questions that are being suggested in "The Power of the Question" are the type that can help you coach someone better. They will also encourage others to coach in a culture of sharing, where it could be everyone's desire to achieve peace, harmony, and understanding.

It has occurred to me that there is a more serious landmine when interrupting the silence after you have asked a powerful question. It has the unintended side effect of seriously derailing the learning process for the other person, no matter their age. Don't do it. [2]

CHAPTER 10

The Power of Words

Not many people are aware that there was a law passed in the US (took effect October 2011) that requires government employees to use Plain Language in writing official documents, instructions and other guidance that is available to the public. Potentially a powerful law that can help us be more effective communicators, this law has no penalties. There is no "Plain language Jail" in which you will be locked up if you violate the spirit and letter of the law.

Nevertheless, words are the means by which our thoughts and hearts and known to others. What do your words say about you? Do you speak plainly or disguise what you mean in lots of words and phrases that are not clear?

Take this self-assessment and ask others to assess you as well. Compare your answers and see if there are any discrepancies between what you think and how others assess your use of language. If you dare, after you have looked at your answers and compared them to others, ask each rater some open questions to tell you more about how they approached this project and what the implications might be for you.

#	Question	Yes	No	Don't Know
1	When I speak, people tend to listen.			
2	I am comfortable sharing my thoughts.			
3	I have hurt others with my words.			
4	I have healed/comforted others with my words.			
5	I tend to talk too much.			
6	I tend to use language carefully.			
7	I am guilty of language pollution.			
8	I don't think too much before I speak.			
9	I have trouble listening carefully when others talk or try to teach me when they use words.			
10	When I am angry, I yell and spew a torrent of words.			
11	When I am angry, I sulk and don't say much.			
12	When I am angry, I journal until I figure out what's wrong.			
13	When I am angry, I pray and stay by myself.			

Take this next assessment to measure what you think others think about how you use words. Often when we think about how others would rate us, we become more insightful and honest. Circle the best answer. It's information that may point out blind spots. Facing them will direct your efforts at self-improvement.

I.   What would my mother say about how I use words?
        i.   I talk too much.
        ii.   I don't talk enough.
        iii.   I talk too fast.
        iv.   I don't think before I talk.

II. What would my father say about how I use words?
        i.   I talk too much.
        ii.   I don't talk enough.
        iii.   I talk too fast.
        iv.   I don't think before I talk.

III. What would my siblings say about how I use words?
        i.   I talk too much.
        ii.   I don't talk enough.
        iii.   I talk too fast.
        iv.   I don't think before I talk.
        v.   I don't know.

IV. What would my favorite teacher say about how I use words?
        i.   I talk too much.
        ii.   I don't talk enough.
        iii.   I talk too fast.
        iv.   I don't think before I talk.
        v.   I don't know.

V. What would my worst teacher say about how I use words?
        i.   I talk too much.
        ii.   I don't talk enough.
        iii.   I talk too fast.
        iv.   I don't think before I talk.
        v.   I don't know.

VI. My biggest problem as a communicator is:

    i.   I talk too much.

    ii.   I don't talk enough.

    iii.   I talk too fast.

    iv.   I don't think before I talk.

    v.   I don't listen carefully.

    vi.   I interrupt others when they are speaking.

    vii.   I don't really care what other people think.

    viii. I don't know.

Key Questions to Consider:

Does the feedback I received indicate that I need to rethink and rescript the words I use in conversation? Do I have the motivation to begin this work? Who can help me?

For specific help, keep reading and dive deeply into the next chapter.

CHAPTER 11

The Power of Arresting, Compelling Language

How many of you, when you speak, notice that your audience hangs on every word you say? I'm sure you'll agree with me that "just because you said something doesn't mean it was heard."

When I had my gall bladder out, I am so glad the surgeon did a laparoscopy, inserting a small camera so he didn't have to hunt around blindly for the organ. He could clearly see what needed to be removed. He thought about the procedure, targeted the organ, marked it, aimed for it, snagged it, and removed it. No doubt about it. It was a gall bladder.

It would have been terrible if the surgeon had hunted around and taken out my upper intestine or appendix instead by mistake.

But how often do we just hurl words around until the other person nods in assent? How many times in that process do we throw garbage in with the good stuff, violating confidences, using language carelessly, hurting people's feelings, and being a general nuisance?

"Learn to use language with the skill of a surgeon."

Use arresting, compelling language, words that people don't expect, and you harness a powerful communication tool. Pay attention to what you say and track the words you use that are trite, too general, and, perhaps, ineffective. If you were to write your words down and then look for weak, boring, and vague language, you could tackle them one at a time and think about replacements. If you overuse phrases and concepts, jargon, acronyms, and buzz words, you will be easier to tune out because your listeners will assume that they know what you are going to say. If your words are predictable, you will be tuned out.

It is said that the mind can process between four hundred and six hundred words a minute. The range of the rate of speech for most Americans is somewhere between one hundred and ten and one hundred and ninety words a minute, depending on where you grew up and what your nationality is.

Do the math. The mind can process more words than anyone can possibly speak per minute. So the mind is bound to wander.

Factor into the communication equation the ways people learn. If you are an auditory learner, you will get more of what any speaker says because you learn by hearing. If you are a visual learner, you will need to take notes and read handouts in order for any learning to take place. If you are an experiential learner, no amount of speaking and note-taking will help you get what someone else is saying. You will need to hear it, read it, teach it, share it, and experience some of it in order for the learning to take place.

When I'm teaching this concept in a classroom, I set the stage for a quick brainstorming session to list more insights into reasons the mind wanders.

I ask, "When you talk, what do most people expect your presentation to be like?" The answers usually come fast and I write on a chart:

Best	Worst
Interesting	Boring
Short	Long
To the point	Irrelevant
Interactive	A data dump
Entertaining	Delivered in a monotone
Relevant	A dull monologue
What I need to know	Has nothing to do with me

Then I write in big letters underneath the "Worst" list: **Violate Their Expectations!**

That's your job; in order to be heard you may need to violate the expectations of those people who are listening to you.

Many people are shocked when I use the word "violate" because that word choice is unexpected and somewhat violent. That's my point. When we use "arresting" language (there I go again), it commands attention and stops listeners from "playwriting," that is writing their responses on the notebook in their minds because they think they know what you are going to say. They tune you out and write their response because listening openly is boring to them.

How you dress your thoughts says a lot about you. You can enhance or damage your credibility and effectiveness by the way you express yourself verbally. If you always wear blue jeans and one day you show up in a great suit, you have my attention. Something is different and I want to know why. The same is true for the language you use.

So using words that people don't expect makes it more likely that you will be heard.

It's important here to set the record straight about some research that has been misunderstood by so many communication teachers. Many consultants quote 7 percent as the rate of effectiveness our words have when we speak. They use that number to imply that our content, the actual words we say, accounts for just a miniscule part of our effectiveness.

When Albert Mehrabian, professor emeritus of psychology in Canada in the 1980s, was researching "first impressions," he came up with that number. He claimed that during a first impression, your "likability" is measured more by body language and your delivery than by your content. But he also found that once you get beyond the first impression, content is very important in the communication process. If you ever had the thought that the actual words you say are not that important, think again.

What would your list look like, the one you are making to reinvent some of your own conversational word choices? Contrast your normal gobbledy gook and boring choices of words with what you "might" say instead.

Words I Used to Say	My Transformed Use of Language
Gee whiz!	I'm astonished!
Old	Experienced
Shut up	Zip it!
Change your thoughts.	Violate expectations.
Exciting words	Arresting language
No one listens.	Just because you said something doesn't mean it was heard.
Something that sticks	It has gription!

In fact, the more you practice inventing new ways to use language, your stock as an effective communicator will increase in value. Dick Foth, a preacher, former college president, and friend, calls some words "accordion words." [1] They include in their meaning so many things. Accordion words are dense with meaning and engage listeners far more than one-dimensional, plastic words.

I recently heard a senior executive describe a project that was not ready for delivery. Instead of saying it was delayed or that someone messed up, he said the project was on "tactical pause." I will not forget that phrase because it is descriptive, it doesn't assign blame to the problem, and it has "gription."

Anthony Trollop, prolific British author of the 1800s, uses language interestingly. He has a phrase I love, "The look unmanned him." Can't you just see someone being shrunk by a look? John Maynard Keynes, British economist, said, "Words ought to be a little wild for they are the assaults of thought on the unthinking."

When you give information to anyone, you have two choices: either you can give new information or you can give a new spin on old information. Giving new information is easier because everyone wants to hear news that is new. New is new and attracts attention just because it is new. Giving a new spin on old information, which is mostly what we do when we communicate, is the hard part. How can you re-explain something in a way that will attract attention and compliance, since it did not on your first, third, or eighth try?

You can use:

- arresting language,
- the power of the **Zip**,
- the power of the question, and
- address the fact that your listeners are asking, "So what, who cares, what does this have to do with me?"

If the arresting language that you devise is memorable, it will be quotable. That means people will not only have heard what you said, but they will want to remember it. If they remember it, they are more likely to comply with what you want from them and then you will have been effective.

At a fashion show in the winter of 2011, I used a "new to others" word to describe a piece of clothing that was out of the ordinary, designed unusually well, and that flattered the wearer in color, style, and fit. All I said was, "Socko!" and the word stopped traffic. People remembered it for hours after I said it. They actually asked where the word came from and I had a chance to describe the Power of Words and what they can do for you. In a gathering of more than ten people, you could hear "socko" being said again and again.

Where did "socko" come from? My ability to think about language in ways that make it useful and memorable produced that word.

Some words stick and some don't. Why have words like "Google," "blog," "Bing," "Facebook," and "Twitter" grabbed hold and become household words? Why did the word "Kijiji" refuse to stick? If you haven't heard of Kijiji, you are like millions of others who have missed it, too. Kijiji was a venture that eBay launched to be a family-friendly Craig's List. The developers put millions of dollars and many years into trying to make the name and the concept stick and, so far, their efforts have failed.

I call the ability of some words to stick and others to limp along "**gription**." Actually, to be completely fair, my third son invented this word. When he was seven or eight, he couldn't think of the word "traction," so out came "**gription**." I tried to interest a few businesses in buying it from us and no one would. But it stuck with me so well that I am now using it here. Let's see how much sticky **gription** the word "**gription**" will have. [2]

When you are attempting to use arresting language, the words that have **gription** need to be repeated. Pay attention to the words that people tune out and remove them from your vocabulary. You will find that you will be heard much more than before.

Think about an important conversation you need to have with someone. It should be a topic about which you have some serious interest. The criterion is that this topic is so important that you need to have the conversation within a week or so or there will be consequences, both visible and invisible.

Write the topic here and try to make your opening remark as arresting and engaging as possible.

_____

_____

_____

Now try to give some feedback to yourself as to how effective this is.

Key Questions to Consider:

Ask yourself:

- How am I using language to engage the other person?
- Am I clear as to what I expect and what steps need to be taken to meet expectations?
- What vague or fuzzy words or phrases could be rewritten?
- Have I addressed what the other person is thinking: "So what, who cares, what does this have to do with me?"
- What other ways can I say this for maximum effect?
- How does it sound to me as I read it aloud?

Rewrite it here: _____

_____

_____

Potential Landmines of Using Arresting, Compelling Language

When you use words that are ordinary, what makes them compelling is how you use them. For example, if you needed to stop a toddler reaching for an electrical outlet, you might shout, "Stop!" The word becomes compelling because of how you say it, the volume, the tone, and the urgency.

As you begin to notice how you say what you say, you will see that certain words have no power to compel someone's attention, and some do. Overusing the words that seem to work will make them lose their power. Save them for the times they are needed. Better yet, speak less and then you won't be overusing your words at all.

The right words are not always enough. We get in trouble if we think the right word will solve every communication problem

Perfection in language is an ideal to reach for. I love the reach. It keeps me mentally stimulated and motivates me to read more and to write more.

My emphasis on using language well might suggest to you that I want us all to become writers and inspiring public speakers, remembered for the words that come out of our mouths. Actually, hearing is not the end product. I believe that we want to be listened to, really heard, and remembered in order to inspire action. That action might be a change of behavior, a change of a mindset, or a change of heart. The transformational power of language is huge and we often fall short.

Kathleen Norris in *Dakota: A Spiritual Geography* has helped me understand my urge to teach, write and mentor others. She overheard some high school students bragging about drinking after a prom and she used this to trump their negativity about writing.

"See, it's like I told you; the party's not over until you've told the stories. That's where all writing starts."

So for me, when I think a new thought, learn something, or experience something that rocks my world, it's not complete until I rock your world. An "aha" moment for me. I love the chase and then I love to share the chase. That completes the experience for me.

What about you? How many people hear words of wisdom, life-altering, transformative, powerful words, and never act on them, in body, mind, or heart?

That's the ultimate peril of the power of words. They may be wasted. Powerful words are a resource that I don't like to squander.

CHAPTER 12

The Power of Truth

The media has an unorthodox approach to the topic of truth. I became aware of this perspective watching the live proceedings of a highly publicized trial. A witness for the defense was recalled because he "misspoke" in previous testimony and wanted a chance to correct the record. Since I watch TV while exercising on a treadmill in my community exercise room and I had lots of time to mull this over, I thought, *What's the difference among the words "misspoke," "misinform," and "lie"?*

I hear these words used so frequently by victims, criminals, elected officials, and spokespersons and I think people delude themselves when they call a lie by another word. If someone lies, then they are not telling the truth. Is there truth or is there only what I know and your truth might be different?

Following this logic, if truth is considered a relative idea, then a lie can also be considered a relative idea.

What hope do we have, when stretching the truth, spinning it, and mangling it is the norm? Advertisers, lawyers, politicians, university professors, the media, and even churches are guilty of this practice of deception.

In all sincerity and simplicity, I am reminded of what I used to tell my children when they challenged me: "If fifty thousand people believe a stupid thing, it is still a stupid thing." [1]

Potential Landmines of Truth

Sticking to the truth can cost you: position, money, fame, fortune, friends, and family. Your values and the fear of suffering such losses will be significant as you wrestle with whether or not to tell the truth.

Many people have lost jobs because they stood up for principles of truth and integrity. It's hard to have integrity when no one around you has it. However, it is not impossible. Courage to assert the truth in a culture where people twist the truth for personal gain, is a rare commodity. I look to role models to help me use the Power of Truth.

Key Questions to Consider:

Who are your role models of people who were not afraid of truth despite potential dire consequences? Do you think you could display the same level of courage they did?

Test yourself in small ways. When someone asks you if you messed up, have the courage to say, "Yes, guilty as charged." Practice telling the truth and you won't need such a good memory," is my paraphrase of Mark Twain's famous guideline. Practice it daily.

It takes courage to believe in the truth, to trust it, and to hold on to it.

How can you live the truth in a world that behaves as though truth were a fashion trend, in and out, up and down like mixing prints and plaids and changing hemlines? One way is to make a list of the truths that are not negotiable for you. Then work it out one decision at a time, one action at a time, one conversation at a time, daily.

CHAPTER 13

The Power of the Physical Setting

First, praise in public; correct in private. If you don't, the wrong setting has the potential to poison the message.

I am always impressed when I see a parent take a child out of a room where there are other people to go to a private room in order to give the child feedback. This is respectful to the child and to the other people. Embarrassing a child with public corrections is unpleasant for everyone.

The same respect should be used professionally, with spouses, and with friends. When my daughter, a professional project manager, calls someone on the phone, she always says, "Is this a good time?" She does it so consistently that it models for me the way she would like to be treated. That question is respectful and other people appreciate that it has been asked. Use it with others and you model how you would like to be treated also.

Creating appropriate space between you and another person prepares a setting of respect and consideration. Whether over the phone or in person, if you initiate the conversation, you can make the physical setting appealing or unpleasant.

There is another aspect of the physical setting that has some power in the communication process. Are you in a dump or a beautifully decorated space? Do you like the colors, the furniture, the sound levels, the lighting, the odors or aromas, and the temperature?

Some people are more stimulated by their surroundings than others. My friend, the actress Florence Stanley (1924–2003), found public settings so fascinating that when we would go out for lunch, her head turned as if it were on a swivel. So if I wanted to have a real heart-to-heart conversation with her, I would visit her backstage in her dressing room, where we could talk undisturbed by others. I did this often when she performed in the Broadway play *Fiddler on the Roof* for five years (1966–1971). She would talk about her ability to be distracted by external stimuli. I don't call it distraction. She was so open to stimuli that the more there was, the more responsive she would be to all of it.

If this tendency to be influenced by outside stimuli is true for you, control the environment where you work or live so that you can do what needs to be done when you are there.

There is an acting technique that can help anyone who feels strange in certain settings, like a dark air traffic control room, or a very bright office with lots of sun glare pouring in through the windows, or a room that is decorated in colors you don't like. Any aspect of what you might consider "unfriendly" in the physical setting of where you work or live or spend lots of time can be countered with this technique.

Look around carefully until you can find one thing or one color or one "anything" that reminds you of something you like. It could be the color lavender, which is hidden in the pattern of the rug, or the scent of perfume that reminds you of your mom's. It might be the shape of a light that reminds you of the shape of something you love in your room at home. Let your mind linger on that search until you come up with one thing. Then, imagine that the thing you love is there in the room with you. This now becomes the trigger that makes you more comfortable, imagining something you like and putting it in the present, even though it is not really there.

Actors use this a lot when they travel from theater to theater and need to connect in a hurry to a new performing space each night. Why can't managers use it when they move from office to office or facility to facility? Why can't people use it when they are on vacation and go from one hotel room to another? Employees who are anchored in small cubicles to do their work could use it to create a sense of comfort and ease for themselves.

If my manager calls me into her office to give me feedback, it will lessen my anxiety if I use this technique to make myself feel more at ease during the conversation.

Potential Landmines of the Physical Setting

If you use the actor's technique of finding something familiar in an unfamiliar place to relate to, there is some peril that you might become so fixated on the comparison that you are not fully engaged in the present conversation or experience. If this happens, it's just because you are unfamiliar with making this "substitution." Practice it and you will discover greater ease in unfamiliar places than before.

Occasionally, you are stuck in a public setting and yet you must give important feedback to someone. Perhaps a child is sobbing because they are hurt, or your teenager has just been outrageously rude, or an irate spouse has just loudly objected to something.

Where you are can make the other person feel horrible, humiliated, embarrassed, or scared. You need to make a choice:

- You can wait until a better time, but you will have lost a teachable moment.
- You can speak softly and hope you are heard by the person who needs to hear you.
- You can ask the person to leave the area with you because of the urgency of the issue.

All of these alternatives are perilous. Which you choose depends on the sense of urgency. I have used each one on different occasions and there is no "one size fits all."

Whether or not you choose the best remedy in the moment, do not despair. I think that's why we love the story of Pinocchio so much. After he confesses his lies to the good fairy, she touches him and he is renewed with more chances. How many chances do you give yourself to improve? How many chances do you give others?

When you reflect on whether or not you've made the right choice and try to learn from the experience, you will be teaching others to do the same. That chance to reflect and learn is the best part of learning to be a more effective communicator.

CHAPTER 14

The Power of Setting Context

Every business and every family has norms or rules about "The Way We Do Things Here." Most are spoken about (explicit) and some are unspoken (implicit).

Where are your business norms written, or are they cultural lore, unwritten but known by all?

Have you ever written the family norms down, in a family handbook, for example? When you stop laughing, consider for a minute that you and (hopefully) your spouse know what you expect. Suppose you and your spouse do not agree on "The Way We Do Things Here." Suppose you are a single parent and you are deviating from the old ways to ways that are different from the patterns you had in your past.

Regardless of your circumstances, you need to know and your family needs to know what your expectations are. Disagreements might be avoided if families could talk about these norms before violating them gets someone in trouble.

For example, in our home when the boys wore baseball caps, and they had scores of them to wear, it was expected that they would remove them at certain times: dinner, while being a dinner guest at someone else's home, in church, and in class at school. Suppose one day one of my boys decided to wear his new hat, properly broken in, of course, to a family meal when guests were invited.

Our conversation might sound like this:

Me: Son, I see you are wearing your new hat. It looks great.

Son: Glad you like it. It took me a long time to break it in just right.

Me: I saw you working on it. I want to talk with you about something that puzzles me. We always have agreed as to the right time to wear a hat and the time when it's just not appropriate. And now we seem to be disagreeing about the appropriateness of wearing a hat at Sunday dinner. Can you tell me what's going on? (Then **Zip it!**)

Son: Well, since we are going with the Smiths to a game after dinner, and since their son, my best friend, also has a new hat, we thought it would be fun to wear them all day.

Me: I see. A fun idea, almost. When you want to do something that is different than what we have agreed on, I need to be asked for my opinion. Is that okay with you?

Son: I don't see what the big deal is.

Me: I know. Let me see if I can explain it. When we agree to do something, I like the security of knowing I can trust you and your brothers to follow family norms unless we all decide to change them.

Son: I didn't think it was that big of a deal.

Me: The hat isn't the big deal. It's the norm about wearing the hat that's the deal.

Son: I can see that.

Me: So what about today and the hat at dinner?

Son: I guess I can take it off and wear it the rest of the time, if it means that much to you.

Me: It means that much to me, the family, the trust part of what we do, and how we do it.

Son: Okay.

Me: Thanks, son, for trying to understand. I appreciate it more than you can know.

In this conversation it was important to set the context. We were talking about the **norm** of hats, not hats. We were talking about the way we do things, security, and trust, not rebelliousness. We were talking about how we do things in this family and why. We were talking about broken agreements and how they should be handled. We were not talking about who has the power, the parent or the child.

When I coach an executive, I need to set context frequently or my coachee won't understand my feedback and coaching questions.

For example, Jessica (the name has been changed) described her dissatisfaction with Joe to me when he made an important presentation to a client without first folding her edits into it. As she described her feelings of being let down, not just this time but on other occasions as well, I was able to help her diagnose a pattern of Joe letting her down.

First, I set context by describing the essence of the book *Crucial Confrontations,* an accountability conversational model to use when people violate expectations.[1] Using that methodology to set context helped her understand how to approach the conversation she was planning to have with Joe. There were two issues to deal with: the problem of the edits and the pattern of behavior of his disregarding her instructions.

Without setting this context, Jessica would risk being perceived as a micromanager and complainer. With this context, she was preparing the groundwork for greater future collaboration.

Second, at the very least, I walked her through the process of how to handle his objections if Joe thinks he can't make the edits because he lacks the time or because of some other barrier. He has to know that the intrinsic value in this company is that "if something comes up, he will let the boss know as soon as possible."[2] Then she would have the option of making the edits herself or delegating the work to someone else.

Common context keeps Jessica and Joe on the same team and minimizes this and future conflicts. Context keeps people talking about the same issue. Without it, she might talk about the slides and he might talk about pressure and lack of time, and the conflict could fester and escalate.

Setting context and being clear as to what you are talking about will prevent arguments and inspire cooperation. In fact, here is a rule. Set context before you share content. That's the best way to insure that you have the listener's attention.

Have you ever worked in an office where any of these scenarios are played out?

- The boss walks in your office and begins to talk, describe a task or ask for work without first setting context
- Your best friend calls you in the morning to complain about something without first saying, "Good morning!"
- Your spouse comes home from work talking about a "situation" without first letting you know what it's about
- You walk over to a secretary and ask for some supplies and are frozen with a look or ignored

All of these events occur because context wasn't set before the person shared content.

It seems clear to me that one reason why heads of state, presidents, and royalty have state dinners, balls, and exquisite protocol displays before actual business and negotiations take place, is because they are setting context first. It's as if they are saying, *This is who I am. I am not just a person. I am the composite of all the protocol and trappings of my position. Please take all of this into account when we eventually have substantive conversations.*

There is a historical marker in a small park on Ox Road in Fairfax County, VA commemorating The Battle of Chantilly. The sign says, "The Death of General Kearney." It might have said "The Life of General Kearney" if an outspoken soldier under his command had set context when he shouted to the General, "Don't go there!"

If instead, the soldier had said, "General, I have information that will be a matter of life or death to you, please listen. Can you stop for a minute," the General might have been a hero instead of a martyr.

Continuing my rewrite of history, if the soldier had set context, he might have blurted, "That cornfield you are about to enter is infested with Confederate soldiers." Then the General might not have been shot like a crow swooping in for dinner. If he had listened, his story might be told with honor in history classes even today.

Instead, his troops were dumbfounded because they found out in a dramatic way that "just because you said something, doesn't mean it was heard."

Darn! Darn about the death of General Kearney. Darn that people don't listen when it could have the power to save their lives.

Landmines We Create When We Don't Set Context

Without context, many conversations would be like a comedy routine, with no one really being clear as to what's being talked about. Worse, without context, many conversations will be power struggles with one person ruling by virtue of the fact that they think they can, and with the other feeling helpless, never heard or understood.

Without context, arguments between husband and wife will deteriorate because each will have his or her own agenda and want to be heard. Each will have trouble listening openly because neither can ever be sure as to what's being talked about.

If you have never read *Crucial Conversations* and *Crucial Confrontations*, this would be a great time to read, digest, and add the techniques they cover to your arsenal of ways people communicate effectively.

CHAPTER 15

The Power of the Bridge

Remember the Simon and Garfunkel song "Like a Bridge over Troubled Water"? That's how we need to behave when there are two opposing views and we want to persuade someone of our view. We need to be like a bridge over troubled waters.

The lyric goes on to say, "I will lay me down." I am suggesting we need to be proactive and cross over to the other side, not lie down so others will walk on us. Here's how this works.

What happens if you sincerely want to persuade someone to change their mind about something? You can say, "Hey, come over here to where I am." What they hear is that where they are is not a good place to be.

What happens when we exhort others in that way is that we fail to make an impact. No one wants to be told that where they are is not a good place to be. So they dig their heels in and stay. The act of staying becomes even more important to them than why they want to stay.

You have behaved that way. We all have.

Now here's the better way. When you want to influence someone to change, first, cross over to where they are. Ask questions; understand what they believe and why they believe it. Understand all the factors that influence them to choose their position. Ask more questions. Imagine you are this person and try to see if there is any way, given their circumstances, that you would hold the same position as they have.

Then, and only then, can you be the bridge that will inspire them to begin to move in another direction.

Me: Thanks for the invitation to go out to dinner at _____. I don't think I will join you because there is nothing on the menu that I can eat.

You: Well, we want to eat here, we were really looking forward to this, and it's a convenient location for us all.

Me: I'm disappointed because I was really looking forward to this occasion. I'm wondering if this is an "all-or-nothing" decision. Are there any other choices possible?

You: Well, actually this is our favorite restaurant. We all love it. We know that you can't find something to eat there and I've called them and they say it's okay for you to bring your own food in. Next time we get together, we'll eat at the place you select.

Me: Well, I'm happy you care for this as much as I do. I'll see if I can get take-out from my favorite place and bring it in. Thanks for making the phone call to get clearance for me on that.

You: You're welcome.

Me: See you at noon.

You: Great. Glad this worked out.

How did this go? I think it went well because it ended up with an agreement and a compromise that was acceptable to both people. The inviters, **"You"** in the above dialogue, wanted me to come over to their side. Where I was, was not where they wanted me to be. Nothing they could do or say would change my position. However, they introduced a choice that showed they honored my position. I could still eat what I wanted to eat without missing the opportunity to be with them. No one's feelings were hurt and there was no power struggle. Each person has a better appreciation of what's important to the other. The next time they discuss a meal, it will be easier to agree on the right thing to do.

In this example, **"You"** acted as the bridge, not a crow bar trying to pry me loose from my position. The result was a win-win for all.

Potential Landmine of Using the Bridge

If you are always the bridge for others, but have no one who serves as a bridge for you, you may begin to feel taken advantage of. That is, until you remind yourself that life isn't all about you. It's about others and how you all interact.

Remember in the beginning of this book I said that our conversations are mostly about the other person, not about us. If that thought has gription in our minds and behavior, we will be better at talking and listening.

CHAPTER 16

The Power of Eye Contact

Eye contact contributes to ease or uneasiness during communication. Are you comfortable looking at someone with a clear gaze? Can you receive their eye contact? Your answers will give you all the feedback you need to assess your own approach to eye contact. You probably already know if you are able to use eye contact well in communicating. So do the people you talk with. If you are uncomfortable, you may be somewhat fearful of public speaking, even if your public is only one person.

If you are uncomfortable with eye contact, it is also possible that you were raised in another country or by people who were raised in another country. Other cultures vary widely from the American value that eye contact is important.

When raising children, from the moment they are born, eye contact is a critical skill that helps normal development. I remember looking at each of my three boys from the moment I first held them in my arms when I was still on the delivery table. My first son had a clear gaze even from the first moment. My second son looked around the room and seemed to be fascinated by light and shadow on his left hand. My third son looked at me and also looked around.

Every day I would spend lots of time, seemingly hours, just looking at each boy, talking, observing, singing, and doing all the things a loving parent does with a baby. Having total eye contact was important to me and I would engage them in the sport of looking. I even had specially designed eye focus graphics, a Fisher Price baby toy, that helped them develop their eye muscles. And I learned to alternate sides each time I nursed them, so that their eye muscles would develop equally.

As the boys grew, many of the things I taught them required eye contact so I could make sure they understood what I was saying.

There is research to support my motherly instincts.

A 1996 Canadian study with three- to six-month-old infants found that smiling in the infants decreased when adult eye contact was removed. [1] A recent British study in the Journal of Cognitive Neuroscience found that face recognition by infants was facilitated by direct gaze. [2] Other recent research has confirmed the belief that the direct gaze of adults influences the direct gaze of infants. [3], [4], [5]

Fast forward to their teenage years when the last thing a normally insecure teenager wants to have is eye contact with an adult. I sent my boys to schools where communication with teachers was very important. I was pleased that the eye contact I had been teaching them at home through my example was reinforced at school.

Today, each is comfortable maintaining good eye contact with other people. To me it appears that they are comfortable with themselves and with others.

Many adults I know have not had such training in childhood or later. Although they are intelligent, good listeners, and interested in other people, they give the appearance of not caring; they look nervous and ill at ease because they lack good eye contact.

If this is an area in which you do not excel, it is possible to reeducate yourself and improve your eye contact. Practice on grocery store cashiers, bank tellers, anyone you encounter and with whom you can have a conversation for a minute or two. Challenge yourself to look at them, not look away, and to relax while you are doing it. If you are still ill at ease, ask a close friend to observe you and give you some feedback.

People with autistic disorders or some form of social anxiety will have difficulty with good eye contact. Telling people whom you must deal with regularly that you have some challenges with eye contact will make you easier to deal with and sensitizes others to work with you gently.

The benefits are huge since the eyes are usually the window into the soul, a traditional proverb of dubious origin, and yet I believe it to be true. Let others in and you will be "known" more intimately, just as you are trying to know those you are close to.

Potential Landmines of Not Using Eye Contact

If you have many cultures at work or in your family, you know that there are many cultural differences relating to eye contact. Along with all the other adjustments that are necessary in cross-cultural marriages, this is another one.

Diversity in the workplace, in particular, mandates that you talk about this and other differences among cultures so that you don't misinterpret someone's lack of eye contact as rudeness or lack of caring. Bringing differences to light provides education for all and improves the quality of life for all at work and elsewhere.

CHAPTER 17
The Power of "Taking In"

There is another power in relationships that is related to eye contact but goes much deeper. I can best describe this using an example from the theater.

When actors study their craft, they practice something called "taking in." That means you "take in" not only what is said and how it's said, but what is not said yet implied. This is not only the body language but the entire emotional, intellectual, sensory meaning, sub-meanings, and the subtext. [1] When you "take in" someone, it's what you sense in the pause that gives you a deeper knowledge of where someone is coming from. It is your discernment that helps you measure a person.

The Broadway play *A Raisin in the Sun* by Lorraine Hansberry deals with this poignantly when the son who wants to get ahead makes poor decisions and the rest of the family has to deal with the fallout. The consequences were once invisible to the son and now are visible to him and to his family. This is the negative result of his poor decision-making. His grandmother makes a plea for the power of "taking in." She is the "manager" of the family relationships and she is compassionate and demonstrates the power of caring.

She says, "Child, when do you think is the time to love somebody the most? When they done good and made things easy for everybody? Well then, you ain't through learning—because that ain't the time at all. It's when he's at his lowest and can't believe in hisself 'cause the world done whipped him so! When you starts measuring somebody, measure him right, child, measure him right. Make sure you done taken into account what hills and valleys he come through before he got to wherever he is" (Act 3, Scene 1, Line 113).

"Taking in" takes into account the hills and valleys someone has journeyed through before they get to this moment in time. The past is not an excuse for not taking responsibility for your actions. The past is a lens that gives the present more clarity and can help chart the course for the future.

Hearing can be both intellectual and spiritual. One level is to have a "hearing heart" or "discernment" or "understanding." Hearing on this level would be "taking in" to your full ability. [2]

People who are not skilled in "taking in" usually miss so much that is going on with other people. Others will say to them:

- You just don't understand.
- You don't see it.
- I feel so misunderstood.
- You are out of touch.
- I might as well be talking to myself.
- My dad doesn't know where I'm coming from and doesn't seem to care.

People that "take in" other people are the best listeners and get more information about what is said and what is unsaid but needs to be said, in order to make better decisions. The power of taking in is that when you do it, the other person feels heard, feels accepted, not necessarily approved of, but valued.

Remember the directive to "use language with the skill of a surgeon"? Well, the match for that in relation to listening is, **"Learn to listen as though every word you hear were the oxygen you needed to breathe."**

Not too long ago I had a student who copied that down after I said it in class and went home and shared it with his wife. Knowing her husband well, she wittily replied, "If that were true, you'd be dead."

When he shared that with me in another class, I roared and asked for permission to repeat it. It makes the point so well. Listen well, or you might suffer!

Potential Landmines of "Taking In"

At home, there doesn't seem to be any downside to "taking in." Parents who do this with one another will naturally do it with their children. It's a skill that can be taught.

If you are uncomfortable with this skill, look for role models to copy.

When I was in professional acting school, The Tisch Graduate School of the Arts at New York University, we worked on "taking in" for our first year, in a class that lasted three hours a day, three times a week. I was probably the worst in the class for this task and my acting teacher, Olympia Dukakis, patiently guided me into its secrets.

I had to learn to accept all of my deep thoughts and feelings before I could discern and accept the thoughts and feelings of others. That was rough since my parents liked to gloss over real feelings or label them something other than what they were. For example, if my mother was furious and yelled and cried, she would tell me, "I'm not angry." That's confusing for a child.

In class, second by second, moment by moment, I had to build up an ability to accept the reality of my feelings. Thanks go to Olympia for not losing heart.

In the workplace, many people do not want to be "known" on a deep level. They put up clear boundaries that should be respected. At home, some families do the same.

You can't rush trust. We are suspicious of people who pressure us into trust and openness before they have earned it. As you become skilled in "taking in," you may know much more than you will share. You will sit on this information and your impressions for a long time to test them. You may never have an opportunity to share all that you have sensed. Your information will simply make you a better person. **Perhaps trust needs to be earned one crisis at a time and you need to respect the distance that some require at first to earn the trust later to build a deep relationship.**

CHAPTER 18

The Power of Patience

Sometimes people cannot zip it, or wait, or take others in because they are not patient. They are highly intelligent, quick-thinking, and an instinctive problem-solver. Every conversation with a peer, child, employee, parent, friend, and even a casual acquaintance is an opportunity to solve a problem, they think.

This may be the only behavior they learned while growing up, solving other people's problems.

When we treat other people in another way, not as a problem to be solved but as an opportunity to let others discover themselves, we need to practice patience, redesign our habits, rethink our behavior, and get out of the way of others. Certainly other people may make mistakes when we have this hands-off attitude. But we have choices. They are:

- To solve others' problems vs. letting them figure out their own solutions
- To enable others and rescue them vs. letting others assume responsibility to figure things out
- To control the outcomes of so many activities vs. relinquishing control and see if others can rise to the occasion

How can we develop the patience and self-control to do this?

Key Question to Consider

When the urge to solve problems, be an enabler, or control things or people becomes overwhelming, what's the remedy? Call a friend who has agreed to hold you accountable; breathe; take a walk; read a book; leave the area; drink a glass of cold water; "Meddling is bad; patience is good." [1]

Potential Landmine of Patience

When we fail to exercise patience, when we fail to overcome our bad habits and slip into our default method of meddling and controlling others, the penalty is almost always negative. We cripple others, keep them dependent on us, and we prove over and over again that we don't know everything. We do this because we are bound to make mistakes.

Patience is not easy but neither is lack of patience. As for me, I prefer the benefits of patience.

CHAPTER 19

The Power of Discernment

The Power of Discernment is connected to the Power of Taking In. Since people and things are often NOT what they appear to be, an educated sense of discernment can save you from making critical errors in judgment that could have dire consequences for team work and harmony.

The type of discernment I'm talking about here has to do with what I have called the "circles of ability." I learned this from South African leadership coach Murray Kilgour. He learned them from Dan Sullivan and they are described in detail in *Unique Ability* by Nomura and Waller. [1]

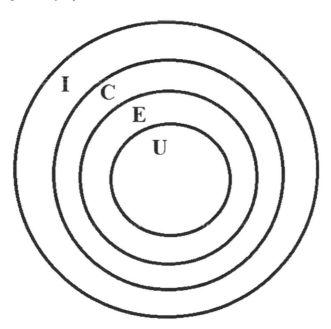

The largest circle is labeled **"I,"** which stands for **incompetence.** All people have at least one area of weakness or incompetence. These are the things you work at that cause you the greatest frustration. Some are no good with numbers and financial planning. Some are not good in the kitchen cooking; some are not good with cleaning. Sometimes we are incompetent at some of the tasks in our job description: manager, employee, parent, son or daughter, sibling, friend.

To be honest we all have at least one area of incompetence and we are best served if we don't mask this from the people we work or live with. If I am ever hired as an accountant, it will be because all the accountants in the world are dead! No joke!

One year I bartered with a friend for cleaning chores in my house. She cleaned my house for half a day. I cooked one dinner a week for her family, with lots of courses and leftovers. She thought she was ripping me off because she wasn't good in the kitchen and didn't like cooking. I was positive I was ripping her off because I hated cleaning. We were both happy because we delegated the tasks related to our greatest weakness so we could spend more time working on our strengths.

If I worked with a master accountant for ten years, I might gain some skill, but I would be miserable because numbers are not my strength. If you work on your areas of weakness for ten years, you will have very strong weaknesses.

The next circle inside is labeled "c" and stands for **competence**. This is not competence with a capital letter, as in that which you can do with great ability. This is the little "c," meaning that you can do the job adequately but you are not brilliant at it. If you are a manager, someone working for you in their "c" is not your "go-to" person. Others can also do this job and this person is average. We may be competent in several areas but when we do this work, it is not fulfilling or gratifying and we may always look for an opportunity to delegate these tasks to others.

The next circle inside is "E," which stands for **Excellent**. When someone is excellent at his or her work, they can get some satisfaction from knowing they are very good. They are so good that bosses, spouses, or children tend to overload the "E"s, and therefore they are in danger of burning out, or, as a colleague tells me, "They will get crispy!"

It's easy to tell who is an "E" because they are the people most likely to have a second job or all-consuming hobby that they can't wait to do at the end of the day, if their workday ever ends. This is because even though their expertise may be formidable, they don't have passion for what they do.

When we do the jobs at which we are excellent, we may feel that others are taking advantage of us. "Why can't they learn to do that? If I help them with that, they may become dependent on me and then I won't have time for the stuff I really want to do."

I was once in a study group with a full-time mother who also wrote science fiction. She would stay up late after the children went to sleep and write three pages per night. She said that after a year, she had a book and several have been published. I'm guessing that parenting was her "C" or "E" because imagining the world of science fiction and writing about it was her "U," her area of unique ability. She needed to write to feel completely fulfilled.

I also knew a mother who pulled an all-nighter once a week. During that time her husband helped with the kids while she caught up on her sleep the next day. But during her all-nighter, she did all the house cleaning, cooked meals for a week, did the laundry, the mending, and the ironing, and generally kept the house ship-shape. That would never work for me, but she said it gave her a sense of fulfillment, which she needed. Mothering was her "E." Home management was her "U."

The middle circle stands for "U." With no exceptions, everyone has at least one area of **unique ability.** When you use this ability, the results are a home run almost every time. When someone who works for you is in their "U," they have great passion for their work; it blows their hair back and floats their boat. It's their major strength, their area of unique ability. When one of your children discovers this early, they are capable of incredible achievements and may be called a genius or prodigy.

If a close friend gets sick and has a long recuperation and you love to cook, you might go to her home for a day or two, cook up a storm, and load up the refrigerator and freezer with weeks of precooked meals because you love it. I have such a friend who worked her cooking and helping mojo after my gall bladder operation and I can still remember all that she did for me. In fact, although I didn't give her any money for her efforts, I'm sure she would have objected because she loves to help out in that way. She was in her "U."

When you are working in your area of unique ability, time flies by. You may miss meals, breaks, and meetings because what you are doing is engrossing, stimulating, and very worth the effort.

In families, discernment will help you figure out which abilities are unique, excellent, competent, or incompetent for each person. If there is a way to give everyone a chance to work in their area of unique ability often, these people will perform at a high standard of excellence because they love what they do. Morale will be high, and the end product will also set the gold standard. Even if you can't do this as often as you like, if you can relate a seemingly meaningless task to the person's area of unique ability, you will have a happy motivated child, spouse, friend, cousin, etc.

This discernment will also be invaluable at work. Managers who assemble teams taking their unique abilities into consideration will improve productivity, morale, and loyalty of each employee.

When people know that their strengths are valued, they will want to try to interpret what they do in light of their strengths and give the best they have to the work they do. It's a win-win for themselves, their family, and community.

So where do you fit on the chart? Successful people, people who think they are successful and radiate that to others, are usually in their area of **unique ability**. If you are not working in your area of unique ability, perhaps this is a season of your life that you need to endure until: you retire, get a new job, divorce, remarry, or until your children get older. In times of economic hunkering down, people who are realists don't complain when they are not working in their "U" because they are grateful to help the mission of their job and their family. This outlook is contagious and will affect the morale of everyone for the better.

If you are not working in your area of unique ability, you may be counting down the days to retirement, even if you will be retiring in six years, one hundred and six days, and seven hours! That's not a good way to live and the stress and dissatisfaction you are experiencing is probably not comfortable.

Sometimes people willingly work at a job that is not in their "U" because they believe a better opportunity will come along and they are willing to wait while they earn a living in a way that doesn't really inspire them.

As you are able to discern where you are and where others are in the circle of abilities, so you will be able to help your co-workers, your employees, your children, your spouse, your friends, and yourself grow realistically and successfully. Managers who know the strengths and weaknesses of each work unit member are more likely to be team players and to celebrate the successes of others and help realign when the weaknesses of others slow productivity down. Acknowledging these realities helps everyone know they have been "taken in," understood, appreciated, and acknowledged for what they do.

Key Questions to Consider:

If you don't know what circle of ability each of your employees or family members is in, how can you find out? Do you know where you are? How can you find out? When you get crabby and what you are doing is not in your area of unique ability, what steps can you take to reframe it in your mind so that it will relate positively to your "U"? Start by buying the book referenced in the footnotes. It guides you through many questions to answer in order to discover your "U."

Everyone has the capacity to access and use their unique ability. But many get distracted by other interests and never fully excel in their area(s) of special giftedness.

Buying the book *Strength Finders 2.0* by Tom Rath enables you to take an online test to assess your top five strengths. [3] On the inside of the book, near the back, is a packet containing an access number that can only be used once, so everyone needs to buy the book for themselves. It's worth it and can be bought in bulk at a discount from bookstores. (Resist buying it used because the access number cannot be reused.)

For me this information has given me freedom that I didn't know existed. Before learning about these tools, I felt that I was like the circus performer who tries to keep eighteen plates spinning at one time. Not really knowing my areas of giftedness, I always worked in many careers simultaneously. It created great stress and I had trouble choosing my area of specialization.

Now, since taking the test, I am experiencing greater freedom in my life and career, not plagued by what else I should be doing. I am making better decisions as to family relationships, friendships, business opportunities, and how I should spend my time. Not only am I amazed but my husband is amazed that the Strength Finders inventory should have made such a difference. I have taken aptitude tests, MBTI, the Insight Inventory, and others before. This is the first time that I have information that resonates within me and has freed me to pursue excellence in my work and life more intentionally.

Potential Landmines of Discernment

Just because you can discern some thoughts, feelings, and attitudes of others doesn't mean you need to discuss these with others or with the person in question. Learning to keep these things to yourself is part of the power of **the Zip.**

A discerning person chooses how much of his or her insight to share. Disclosing insights to others who are not ready to hear what you know can damage relationships and self-esteem. It is better to share discernment with an eyedropper rather than a fire hose. People need time to hear, understand, digest and wrap their minds around deep truths.

CHAPTER 20

The Power of Hospitality

The concepts of diversity and tolerance have replaced the idea of "America as a melting pot." Instead of respecting the idea of assimilation, we seem to value diversity more. In the United States of America, we know that there is tremendous diversity among our citizens. Visit Oregon, Alabama, New York, Nebraska, and Florida just to get started appreciating the varieties. Twenty-five years ago the public school where two of my sons attended grade school sent home announcements to the parents in 17 languages.

Multi-ethnic, multi-lingual, multi-religious, multi-generational, and with more lifestyle possibilities than were ever dreamed of even fifty years ago, citizens everywhere need to be more hospitable than ever before. Accommodating individuals is definitely not one size fits all. If we reframe our thinking to accept that each group and subgroup, each individual, is so unique that making room for the diversity needs to be the norm, we will practice the Power of Hospitality and be obvious role models to others.

An example that makes this point dramatically is the diversity of food preferences people have. No cafeteria could possibly meet the requirements of every diet, and even having a pot luck meal can pose problems for a host who wants to try to meet everyone's nutritional and dietary needs and wants. Consider the task of bringing a snack or birthday treat to your child's school. You have to be sensitive to allergies: gluten, peanuts, sugar, dairy, chocolate, and other foods.

Registering for special airline meals highlights the ultimate in the power of hospitality. On British Airways, for example, the dietary choices include:

- Baby
- Bland
- Child
- Diabetic
- Fruit platter

- Gluten-free
- Hindu
- Kosher
- Lacto ovo vegetarian
- Low-calorie
- Low-fat
- Low-lactose or lactose-free
- Low-sodium/salt
- Muslim
- Seafood
- Vegan vegetarian
- Vegetarian Hindu
- Vegetarian Jain

I'm sure they have left something out in this list, like the Weight Watchers® and Jenny Craig® cuisines. To practice the Power of Hospitality, the sheer volume of choices can seem overwhelming.

Diversity has stretched people worldwide to practice hospitality to others in ways that have never successfully been done before in the history of the world. Societies were so much more homogeneous.

Practicing the Power of Hospitality is not limited to travelers. Workplaces are rightly challenged to become more hospitable to a very diverse workforce and so are our schools, families, churches, and other community groups. If someone in your family can't navigate the steps in front of your home, wouldn't you want to build a ramp? The etiquette of hospitality varies from place to place all over the world. It may be challenging to practice all of the nuances, but it sure is obvious when hospitality is missing.

When teaching managers from the TSA and the FAA, I have always been impressed by the students from Hawaii. Ninety-nine percent of the time, they arrive in class with boxes of macadamia nuts with and without chocolate, as well as other treats. They packed their bags risking overweight charges just to bring a bit of the island hospitality to the class. It's part of their culture and they can't seem to live without it. They place such a strong value on the Power of Hospitality that they bring it with them.

A manager wrote this for me to share with you about "island culture":

"We from Hawaii believe in spreading the 'Aloha' by bring gifts everywhere we travel. Whenever I attend management meetings and training courses, I bring macadamia nut chocolates. If I'm aware that someone doesn't eat chocolates, I bring them macadamia nuts. I bring one hundred percent Kona coffee for those that I know are coffee drinkers.

"Every year I give Hawaiian pictorial calendars, particularly to administrative personnel so whenever I call them, I get VIP service.

"Whenever VIPs come to Hawaii, I meet them at the gate and present them with Hawaiian lei. I chauffeur them to their appointments, handle all their accommodations, and take them to dinner for their entire visit. That's the type of hospitality we provide—a hallmark of our island culture.

"I usually take extra bags or luggage just for bringing the gifts of 'Aloha' and tastes of the islands."

What do the other students bring? Nothing that comes in boxes and is sweet to eat.

In the words of Arthur Amiotte, a Lakota Indian artist, hospitality is "an act of giving which enables the human spirit." I think you find out more about yourself by exceeding your normal giving.

The other startling behavior that I have noticed is that the students from New York City take up a collection at the end of the class to give a tip, a gratuity, to the cafeteria staff. No other group from any other part of the US has ever thought of it or tried to get others to contribute in my experience. We think of New Yorkers as rude and uncaring, but this behavior really violates that stereotype. In fact, it is a demonstration of hospitality to recognize the work others do.

Potential Landmines of Hospitality

Excelling in hospitality can cost you time, money, emotions, privacy and quiet time. When you offer hospitality to others, what you give depends on what they need, not on what you feel like giving. Know this in advance before you start measuring your generosity with an eye dropper. Hospitality measured is, in my opinion, stingy and selfish.

Key Question to Consider:

The opposite of hospitality is also rudeness. Is it ever okay to be rude to others?

We may think that our efforts are of no value and that thought may keep us from being hospitable to others. If that's the case, consider the example of Chen Shu-chu.

On May 10, 2010, *Time Magazine* published their list of the hundred most influential people in the world. My favorite is Chen Shu-chu, cited for her "small, extraordinary acts of kindness."

A vegetable vendor in a market in southern Taiwan, she has made an ordinary, modest living all her life. Yet, she has donated the equivalent of $320,000 to several non-profits. A children's fund, a library, and an orphanage all received Chen Shu-chu's donations.

The article goes on to quote her saying, "There isn't much to talk about, because I did not enter any competition… I haven't really made any huge donations."

To sum up her philosophy of giving, she said, "Money serves its purpose only when it is used for those who need it."

I'm guessing that according to *Strength Finders 2.0*, her strengths include "futuristic" or "connectedness," giving generously to others with no thought for self because helping others was the most important thing to her. She accepted who she was, didn't worry about who she wasn't, and spent her time using her unique ability to help others.

CHAPTER 21

The Power of Vocal Tone

What does your voice sound like: a raspy fog horn, booming, timid, sultry, nasal, throaty, shrill, or hard to hear? If you don't know, do some easy market research.

We have all heard a parent's voice yelling at children with and without this "loving vocal tone."

Which would you rather listen to? Which would you rather use? How can you tell whether or not your vocal tone is loving or not?

Key Questions to Consider:

Here are some questions to ask both yourself and others:

1. When I speak, do you ever say to yourself, *I wish you sounded different?*
2. When I speak, do you ever tune me out because something about my voice is annoying? (quality of voice, not content of what I am saying)
3. Does my voice remind you of someone else? Who?
4. If you were to describe my voice in three words, what would they be?

Listening to the answers may give you some good clues as to what your vocal tone is like. If you don't think the answers put your voice in a positive light, you may want to learn more about how to use your voice.

A more formal assessment follows.

Voice Improvement Assessment	Strongly Agree	Neutral	Strongly Disagree	Never Thought about It
1. I like my voice.				
2. Others say they like my voice.				
3. I almost never experience vocal strain.				
4. If I speak for several hours per day, I experience vocal strain.				
5. Occasionally I get hoarse a few times a year.				
6. Some people have suggested my voice would be good for commercials and/or narrations.				
7. At the end of a day of speaking, I often experience discomfort in my jaw, tongue, throat, stomach, knees, legs, head, or other area.				
8. When speaking, I often run out of air and have to gulp or gasp or recharge somehow to get through what I have to say. I am also often asked to repeat things.				
9. I am often asked to repeat what I say either because of accent or dialect issues.				
10. When I am teaching or sharing in small groups, I "give" more than "take."				
11. Sometimes people say that I have an "attitude"; I am not aware that I do.				
12. I think my intentions are occasionally misunderstood when leading meetings or teaching.				

If you get ratings mostly in the "strongly agree" column for numbers 1, 2, 3, and 6, you probably have a pleasing vocal tone and that's good. That means that people don't usually tune you out because they don't like the sound of your voice. Make the most of that asset and volunteer to do briefings because your voice works for you.

If you answered "strongly agree" for numbers 4 and 5, you may have a raspy, throaty voice, which indicates strain in the throat. You may be tightening the muscles around your neck and the vocal chords to sound more authoritative. It doesn't work. All it does is give you vocal strain and potentially create nodes on your vocal chords, which inhibit their potential to vibrate when you speak.

If you answered "strongly agree" for number 7, there is something wrong and a physician or speech pathologist could give you a specific diagnosis.

If you answered "strongly agree" for number 8, you may not be using the most useful kind of breathing for speaking. The military used to train their ranks to use muscle power for chest breathing, called upper thoracic breathing. All that does is help you to stick your chest out. But it discourages you from making the connections for lower body involvement in the breathing process, which is more helpful.

If you answered "strongly agree" for number 9, and if you want to do something about it, seek a voice coach who can help.

If you answered "strongly agree" for numbers 10, 11, and 12, your vocal tone may be giving a message that you do not intend. Ask others if they think you have a hidden agenda. Are you perceived as angry, disrespectful, rebellious, or other attribute that you do not intend? If so, videotaping yourself to see and hear what others see and hear may be useful.

If you want to know more about this, consult the book *Freeing the Natural Voice* by Kristin Linklater. I was fortunate to study with her and Rowena Balos for a year at New York University and I was able to retrain my voice from hoarse and nasal to a more full-bodied, resonant sound. [1] If you have serious concerns about your voice, look for someone trained in the Linklater Technique in your city. [2] Also contact any professional theater near where you live to see if there is an Alexander-Technique-trained teacher who gives coaching. [3] Since the Alexander Technique helps people figure out where they are tense, this information will help you breathe more fully and improve your voice.

Writer Barbara Jepson, in a "cultural conversation" with Steve Reich, [4] highlights some qualities of the voice that are beyond description. "All the synthesizers in the world can't compare to the richness of human speech as a sound source," says Mr. Reich. "A recording of your voice, my voice, is as much as who we are as a photograph. Maybe more."

The sentiments of two small girls who were remembering their mom who had died a few years before stays in my memory. "Mom had a pretty voice that made you feel warm and safe." I was channel surfing so I don't remember the name of the movie but I do know I saw this on the Hallmark Channel. If a mother's voice can make a child feel warm and safe, what effect does a different voice have on a child? I'm not saying that a woman is unqualified for motherhood if she has an unappealing voice. I am saying that we need to be aware of the effect our voice has on others so we can decide if we are satisfied or need to make some adjustments.

In *Bringing Up Bebe: One American Mother Discovers the Wisdom of French Parenting*[5], Pamela Druckerman describes how a French mother in a playground taught her a parenting secret: the effect appropriate vocal tone can have on children's behavior. Sitting on a park bench with this woman watching their children play, Ms. Druckerman confessed that she didn't know how to get her young son to listen to her. With coaching, she changed her vocal tone from tentative and weak to convincing and solid. In amazement, she was able to stop her son from wanting to run outside the gate by changing her vocal tone. She relates that after only four tries, her son began to play by himself and she had time to talk with her friend.

In this case the American mother didn't understand that it was only her vocal tone that stood in the way of successful parenting. How many of us are unaware of the way others hear us?

Our attitude also affects our vocal tone. Psychologists and writers frequently refer to the classic categories of "happy, sad, glad, and scared." Like the outdated food pyramid of the right foods to eat for health, these feeling words seem to be the major categories that are used to help others detect and diagnose their feelings.

I'd like to add one more: "bad." That's not a feeling; it's an impulse to indulge in behavior that is outside the norm. Everyone has some bad behavior they indulge in when temptation is strong enough:

- Cursing at drivers on the road who cut you off
- Not giving back unearned change at the cash register when the cashier makes a mistake
- Pushing ahead in line

- Switching tags in a store to get a discount on non-discounted clothing
- Drinking alcohol until you are sick
- Teasing someone excessively
- Playing pranks when they may not be welcome

The list could go on for pages.

What are your behaviors that you think are "bad," the things you do that if caught would make you embarrassed or worse?

What are the triggers that you experience that lead to bad behavior so that you are prone to say, like Bart Simpson, "I don't know! I don't know why I did it, I don't know why I enjoyed it, and I don't know why I'll do it again!"

Whether we are feeling happy, sad, mad, scared, or are behaving badly, our actions are fed by our emotions and they feed our voices that affect others. Actors know this and their ability to allow vocal tone to affect how they say what they say creates interesting vocal tones when they speak.

It is the same with non-actors except they are less aware of the subtleties that others will hear. So you may create an effect or a feeling in others that you don't intend simply by your vocal tone. Awareness of this can help you be more effective when you speak. Blind to your vocal tone, you can create barriers between you and someone else.

If you lack warmth in vocal tone, you can compensate for this by using expressive adjectives and adverbs to add feeling words to your conversation. This is important because communicators need to express feelings and to help create feelings in others for true intimacy.

The point is that if you have a vocal tone that is not in harmony with how you feel, you can still make up for it by your word choice. You can always say, "I know that my voice does not sound compassionate and heartfelt, but I want to assure you that I have strong feelings right now. Please know that I am touched by what you are feeling and sharing with me and if I knew how to change my vocal tone, my voice would be more expressive."

Potential Landmines of Vocal Tone

I know some pretty smart people who speak in a monotone and yet have soaring intellects and a good sense of humor. You just wouldn't know it by vocal tone alone.

I also know someone who is brilliant in international reconciliation and yet laughs inappropriately, by her own admission.

It is not always true that a faulty vocal tone means that the speaker doesn't care or lacks intelligence or emotional depth. If I am coaching someone and assess that there is a gap between their feelings and their vocal tone causing the other person to be frequently misunderstood, I will initiate a conversation about words and how we say them and ask some open questions to gauge if the other person is aware of the gap.

If you are aware that your vocal tone conveys a message that you do not intend, mention it up front when you are having professional, reasoned conversations with others. It helps to set the context that there is a gap between who you are and the way you sound, at least that's what other people have told you. It will help others be more receptive to what you say. You have a better chance of being heard.

CHAPTER 22

The Power of Breathing

What is the most useful kind of breathing for a pleasant, user-friendly speaking voice? I will try to simplify this information so you can use some of it without having to hire a vocal coach.

Every bone in the body has the potential to vibrate when you speak. If you were to put your hand on a guitar or piano when it is played, you would feel vibrations. The body is like the musical case and the bones of the body, some 206 (experts disagree as to the precise number), have the potential to vibrate as air and sound come out of the mouth.

Becoming aware of this, you can work to increase the amount of vibrations you feel and that others will hear as you speak. Try this while working out: walking, running, lifting weights. When you breathe out, try to see how many sections of your body are affected by vibrations. Breathe in before doing a particular action; then breathe out while doing the most forceful part of the action.

If you don't feel any vibrations, your voice is probably thin and not very vibrant. If you are aware of the vibrations, where are they: the chest, the pelvic area, the backs of the shoulders, backs of the knees, or front of the face?

There is a technique you can practice to feel the vibrations in the front of the face. The kind of voice that resonates easily there is one people like to listen to.

Make a sound like a motor boat by putting your lips together and blowing through them. If your lips stay together and you are expelling air through them, you will probably make a continuous sound of "b's." Kids like to do this for fun. If you can keep the b's going, breathing and refreshing the impulse to make this sound, you will begin to be aware of vibrations in the front of the face. Keep this up for a few minutes and the sensation of vibrations in the front of your face will be memorable. Your skin will feel a little itchy and you will be buzzing with vibrations.

You have now experienced what Kristin Linklater calls "the forward placement of sound." If you can experience some vibrations in the front of your face when you speak to a group of people, your sound will easily move from you into the room and people will be able to hear you even though you are not using a microphone.

Another type of vibration comes from your middle.

If you are aware of feeling vibrations in your "center," that is somewhere behind the belly button, deep inside your "core" (a Pilates exercise term), you probably have a deeply resonant voice and people also like to listen to voices that are produced this way.

If you have no idea what I'm talking about and you want to improve your vocal tone, research the Linklater Technique and Alexander Technique and try to experience at least one session with a qualified coach. The payoff for you personally and even professionally will be significant.

Potential Landmines of Breathing from Your Center

Breathing effectively has no perils. It contributes to the sounds you make and helps them be clear, resonant, and filled with meaning. The peril comes from not being aware of how important breathing is in the speaking process. The worst that can happen is that your voice will improve and your co-workers, family, and friends will be less likely to tune you out because of your voice.

If however you take a breathing text book and try to work through it by yourself, there is a chance that you could become light-headed and feel or actually become faint. Let someone knowledgeable show you the process first before you solo.

CHAPTER 23

The Power of Articulation

Key Questions to Consider:

Do people understand you when you speak? How is your articulation? How many times are you asked to repeat yourself? Did the people who raised you have any speech or hearing impairments?

If you have received feedback that your articulation is not clear, or if you merely suspect that is the case, you do not have to be handicapped by your challenges.

Articulation problems could be caused by a lisp, a lazy tongue, a stutter, frozen lips, a uvula that is too large and takes up too much space in the back of your throat, or a tongue that is attached too tightly to the floor of your mouth. The lips, tongue, and back of the throat shape our vowels and consonants. Many people overuse their jaws, thinking that opening the mouth wide and then pressing down on the jaw will help them speak more clearly. This is not true and can actually contribute to a disorder called TMJ, thermo-mandibular jaw. It hurts and can cause your jaw to "pop."

A visit to a speech coach or pathologist will give you the correct diagnosis. The rest is up to you.

The Oscar winning Best Picture for 2010 was *The King's Speech*, an informative depiction of how an inspired vocal coach can help someone speak better. As I watched the unorthodox techniques that Mr. Lowe used, I felt like a kindred spirit. I have trained over six thousand actors and thousands of managers and government leaders to use their voices more effectively, and some of my techniques are equally as unusual.

There was the actor I coached who didn't respond to my words. Standing in the back of a Broadway theater, I jumped up and down, waved my arms, laughed, dissolved into despair, rebounded with joy, all non-verbally. That kind of coaching worked for him and his acting improved tremendously.

There was the actor who was able to become more emotionally involved in her work when she made every feeling into a physical activity. I will never forget how she transformed from average to spellbinding.

There was the person who had a lisp, who practiced tongue exercises until his tongue was as limber as a gymnast's torso and he transformed his lisp into clear pronunciation.

There were several children who didn't use their tongues for the "l" sound. The word "hold" became "hoad." Patiently, as I demonstrated the tongue exercise from *Freeing the Natural Voice*, each child repeated it over and over. They would forget to use that tongue when saying words with an "l" in the middle of them, but I didn't despair. One of those boys is now twenty-nine and says "hold" correctly. Another is seven and has mastered the technique.

There was the engineer that I was hired to voice coach because if he didn't improve his articulation, he would never be promoted. What a shame since he was brilliant at what he did!

I worked with him patiently for eight sessions and he tape-recorded them all so he could practice under my guidance at home. I've never seen anyone work as diligently and as hard as he did and the payoff was real. He improved and began a process that he can follow for a lifetime of improvement.

My parents always insisted on clear pronunciation of words as I was growing up. I didn't know that I had a well-developed skill until there were uses for it that made me stand out. I entered and won or placed in many speech contests in high school. My school had no award for public speaking at graduation until I came along. Not an athlete, not the most popular, not the best actress, I could talk well. So they created the Oratorical Award in my graduation year for the first time.

Since then, I have taught thousands and recorded my voice for commercials, hundreds of e-learning programs, and many documentaries, including *Mother Nature* for the Discovery Channel.

Potential Landmines of Articulation

Substandard articulation can hinder your adult life if you are not understood when you speak. Children in school can also be misdiagnosed as unable to excel, when in fact some voice improvement lessons would repair the problems. There is help available so I recommend getting started to change what can be changed. Speech therapists, acting coaches, even discerning friends can help.

Then there is the old-fashioned method. Sydney Poitier, the famous actor who starred in *In The Heat of the Night*, *Blackboard Jungle*, *Lilies of the Field*, and *Guess Who's Coming to Dinner*, was born in the Caribbean. When he came to the US in the 1950s, he worked as a busboy in NYC restaurants. He knew he needed to change his accent to be clearly understood and to succeed as an actor, so he bought a portable radio and would listen to it on a park bench when he was not working. He copied news broadcasters, listening and repeating what they said and how they said it. [2]

Many immigrants from Asia have told me they use the same technique at home copying the news broadcasters they see and hear on TV. It works.

Sometimes if you improve your speaking so that you no longer sound like the people you grew up with, you may encounter criticism or jealousy. They may be thinking, "Who does he or she think they are, sounding so hoity toity with that fancy new way of speaking?" Or you may just think that they are thinking that. Either way, thoughts like that mess with your mind and can minimize your effectiveness as a communicator.

CHAPTER 24
The Power of Mannerisms

Mannerisms are the unconscious or conscious habits many people display when they speak. Some are endearing and some are not. If you watch TV news anchor people, you will see within seconds that they raise their eyebrows, creating a few wrinkles in their foreheads regularly, as a trained habit to give emphasis to what they say. They also lean in and pull back regularly for further interest and emphasis. The public has come to accept these habits as normal and desirable and media coaches train their clients to do these things.

Mannerisms that you plan to display are usually done for emphasis. Some people are fascinating to watch because of their little habits. People that are interesting this way attract attention almost as much for their habits as for what they say. They have a lot of influence over others because people can't take their eyes off of them.

Think of some famous people you admire and try to determine if they have any mannerisms that contribute to their effectiveness. Reese Witherspoon tucks her tongue behind her teeth and giggles sometimes. This is appealing. When Cher was younger, she would toss her straight hair back when she sang, and it made her seem confident. When Oliver North was on TV a lot, conservative and liberal women seemed to fall in love with him because when he raised his eyebrows, he looked like a vulnerable young man. Harrison Ford has perfected the "fearful" look on his face that spells danger, yet danger that he is capable of conquering.

I have several Scandinavian friends who have the habit of gulping air when they speak. Perhaps it's a cultural habit. I find it endearing, not annoying.

When I visited India twice in 2006, I was struck by a habit many Indians practice, the habit of shaking their heads from side to side. The more relaxed they are and the more they like you, the more they seem to do it. I found myself doing it, too, just to be friendly. It is hard to stop.

Key Question to Consider:

How can you know if you have any positive or negative mannerisms? Ask others, if you dare.

Potential Landmines of Mannerisms

Can mannerisms be changed? Yes, if you want to. First you have to know if you have any. Second, pay attention to your body while you speak and catch yourself doing "it."

A videotape will not help here, in my opinion. It will only make you self-conscious. This is the kind of habit you need to self-diagnose with a kinesthetic awareness of your body. Once you have discovered a mannerism that needs changing, it could take up to forty days to change it.

Is it worth it? Have you wondered why you are not more effective at work or with your friends?

I used to lick my lips so much that I was constantly applying lip balm in public. Besides the uncomfortable condition of chapped lips, it was annoying to me that I did this and yet I couldn't seem to stop. I paid close attention to it and was able to ditch the habit within a few months. This was years ago and I still remember it because I had one class that bought me many containers of lip balm as a present. It was both funny and not so funny and I felt that it was a distraction for the students.

If you have mannerisms and people talk about them, they are getting in the way of your ability to communicate with others. Some mannerisms take away from your credibility and your authority.

Many people are controlled by unconscious mannerisms they do not intend. And they are so unconscious that they are shocked when they are pointed out.

For example, some people play with their keys when they speak, which is the best reason vocal coaches suggest speakers empty their pockets before they go on stage.

I was asked to observe a national spokesperson give an important address to a group of about two hundred people. After the presentation, he said, "Okay, Coach, how did I do?" I simply asked in return, "What's with the keys?" He countered with, "What keys?"

He had no idea that he had methodically removed each key off his key ring while he was speaking and then, as methodically, he replaced them, one by one, back on the key ring. We were both stunned at this unconscious habit.

Although you may not be aware of what you do when you speak, others surely are. Make sure you know what they see and hear. (I once worked with a co-facilitator who "snorted" while teaching, due to an uncontrolled post-nasal drip. It annoyed some students and yet this facilitator was not keen on fixing the problem.)

When mannerisms or personal habits affect your paycheck, I assume you will become more curious about them and want to change them. When these mannerisms keep children away from you, when you see them giggling and pointing and even imitating you, it is time to take another look at what you do.

CHAPTER 25

The Power of Facial Expressions

Have you noticed that some people's faces are so interesting to watch because you seem to see what they are thinking and some of what they are feeling? Others have faces that are like stone walls, registering nothing. You have no idea what they are thinking or feeling. These people make excellent investigators, undercover intelligence workers, and poker players. They are not as effective as managers, parents, best friends, or a spouse, who must excel in people skills.

My background in the performing arts is very useful here. An actor may know what to do, how to do it, and have superior intelligence. But unless he or she is interesting to watch, they will not make a good actor. The actors with box office appeal and huge fan clubs are those who are the most interesting to watch. It's hard to quantify this, but when someone has thoughts and feelings and they convey them with appropriate body language, vocal tone, and "heart," they will always compel attention.

Key Question to Consider:

Do you compel attention? Are there barriers that get in the way so others don't want to keep paying attention to you? Check your facial expressions and if there are none to observe, figure out why.

I have a friend, a retired US Marine, whose face looks like the proverbial Marine Corps poster. Bone structure, steely gaze, immovable concentration and focus—they're all there. Professionally, when he manages others, he has to take special care to smile, crack jokes, and twinkle his eyes to make sure others know he is a real person, not a robot marine.

A class I taught that is designed to help managers figure out blind spots that get in the way of them managing effectively stands out in my mind because of a particular student. From day one, he asked each other participant (twenty) and instructor (two) if we perceived him as intimidating. "Do you think I look intimidating? If so, why?" He asked each person this same question a few times and by the end of the class, he had decided by the feedback he received that he "looked" intimidating to others.

So on the last day of class, he got down on the floor and started singing, "I've got sunshine on a cloudy day..." [1] As we looked in amazement, we saw he had a big smile on his face that showed teeth. [2]

He figured out that people rarely saw him smile and when he did smile, his mustache that bordered the laugh lines below his lips hid the expression. People thought he was too serious, no fun, and therefore intimidating. On this day, he dared to change his image and the class loved it. We all encouraged him to bring this "renewed person" back to the office.

Was this a totally new man? No, he just decided to show another dimension of who he was to others. All people are three-dimensional but don't always choose to show these dimensions to others.

We call cartoons one-dimensional because the characters they portray are defined by one characteristic and that gives them little depth. People act like cartoon characters when they are defined by one characteristic and refuse to show more. This damages their effectiveness and limits their role with others.

People who seem to be one-dimensional are predictable. You know what they are going to say, how they think, and how they tackle problems. Their word choice is the same, day in and day out, and their topics of conversation are also predictable. If you are perceived as three-dimensional, you probably live in the present, are somewhat unpredictable, and others enjoy being with you.

Habits and Mannerisms to Change

Old	New
Serious look, wrinkled eyebrows	Open face, relaxed forehead
Leg jiggling or finger tapping	More awareness of breathing and total body involvement in breathing
Lips look "pursed" when thinking	More relaxed lips when thinking in public arena
Monotone	More varied vocal tone
Sloppy clothes	More crisp, laundered, professional clothes
Few facial expressions	A conscious effort to smile and look interested
Add yours here:	

Potential Landmines of Facial Expressions

If you have perfected the art of not letting others know what you are thinking and feeling, we say you have the "mask of attention," even though your mind is many miles away. You may not like to share your thoughts and feelings outside a very small intimate circle of people.

Where is it written that you can't show or share some of what you are feeling so that others know you are human? Likewise, when good news is conveyed, where is it written that you can't experience some joy, smile, and share some of this elation so that you become more "known" to others?

Consider what would happen if you changed the mental model you have of how your face should look.

Even the queen of England, Queen Elizabeth II, a woman not known for public displays of emotion, finally succumbed to the clamor of public opinion and visited Princess Diana's tributes of flowers and notes that adorned the streets of London everywhere soon after her death. That gesture endeared her to many who thought she was not a feeling person. She looked sad and interested and her loyal subjects were reassured that their queen was a real, thinking, and feeling person.

It is written nowhere except in the book of lies you tell yourself that:

- I look ugly when I cry or laugh.
- No one cares about my feelings.
- If I show my feelings, my family will show all their feelings and we will all be emotional wrecks.

If your facial expressions are basically stoic and others can't tell what you are thinking and feeling by how you look, you are telling others that you don't want to be "known." This can prevent your relationships from having depth.

One way you will know if this is true for you is if people often tell you, "I can never tell what's going on with you, your thoughts and feelings." People who have perfected the inexpressive face may have been hurt sometime in their lives. If being open and vulnerable in your past brought you pain, it will be hard for you to reestablish trust and show your feelings. But it can be done.

CHAPTER 26

The Power of Energy

Lehr and Schwartz have written a very useful book called *The Power of Full Engagement: Managing Energy, Not Time, Is the Key to High Performance and Personal Renewal.*[1] In it they talk about four states of energy that people display in the workplace and elsewhere: high and low negative and positive energy. They also refer to physical, mental, emotional, and spiritual energy and how that affects other people.

All states of energy are contagious and you may experience many waves of energy in every category even before you get your second cup of coffee, tea, diet soda, or bottle of water. You walk into work with high positive energy because you are a morning person, have already been to the gym, and you are ready to tackle your first project. Then you discover that you have been reassigned to other work with someone you don't like. Immediately you may dip into low negative energy. Then some co-workers show up and they are discussing their reassignments and everyone begins to get angry. This feeds on itself and in a minute or two you are all in a high state of negative energy, complaining and planning how to get management to listen to you. In the next minute you discover that you misunderstood the reassignment and you are actually working on something that has always interested you. Your favorite co-worker is the team lead. You become mellow, have a meeting to plan the project, and quietly get to work.

You have experienced four states of energy in a short time and you might be exhausted.

The high and low states of negative and positive energy are fairly easy to recognize, unless you have a serious blind spot and can't tell if you or others are depressed. In my opinion, that's the most critical state to pay attention to. People who are depressed or consumed with depressing thoughts have the potential to cause violence in the workplace. We don't need another Oklahoma City, Columbine, Virginia Tech, 9/11, postal, Norwegian, or Arizona incident to jolt us out of complacency. Be on the lookout for anyone who is depressed and won't talk about it or get help. You may have to get help to deal with this kind of individual before it's too late.

How do you handle a child who doesn't get their way and pouts and sulks and throws toys in their room? Do you match them negative energy for negative energy? Since I have told you that all states of energy are contagious, when everyone else thinks they are in a war zone, someone needs to be in a safe zone, calm, reasonable, and available for peace talks. That would be you. Your name is on that one. Whether or not you feel like it, act like a reasonable, calm person and you will become one.

I have seen a calm manager have a transforming effect on an emotional employee who was upset about something. I have seen a parent do the same with an out of control child. With a calm vocal tone, a steady presence, and determination to make a difference, a person can influence a person with negative energy to want to change their attitude for positive energy.

Key Questions to Consider:

What would your life be like if you made time to **exercise** almost daily? Is getting up twenty minutes earlier worth it?

How did the last book you **read** enrich your thought life? Are there books to read that are stacked in a pile that need to be looked at and used? Can you enrich your time on a treadmill or elliptical or stationary bike by listening to audio books? What about time spent waiting for kids at a sports practice or doctor's office?

Are you hungry, angry, lonely, or tired most of the time and self-medicate with food, drink or other substances? Al Anon uses the acronym **HALT**, which can help you self-diagnose when you need "a timeout." Many people say, "I'm always hungry, angry, lonely, and tired!" If that's true, "take time apart before you come apart." You know the adage that even if you don't have time to do things right now, you will have to take time to fix them when they break. **Fix yourself, before you are required to take a sanity break.**

What about your spirit? Who are you when no one is looking? What are your **values** and how do you recharge them? If you don't have time to think about that, you are fooling yourself if you think others can't tell. Do you arrive late to work and leave early? Do you only think about receiving instead of giving? When you see trash on the ground instead of a receptacle or on your front lawn, do you pick it up or walk by? What about a messy bathroom at home or in a public mall or restaurant? If you are getting off an airplane, do you help someone get their bag down from the overhead compartment? At the grocery store, do you help someone load the contents of their cart onto the conveyor belt if their kids are acting wild?

Potential Landmines of Energy

Without energy, we would be dead. So energy is required for life to exist.

I once co-taught a class with a man who was very self-contained and did not display many emotions. He always appeared to be calm, with low positive energy. That must have been an asset to him in his former career in law enforcement.

To understand this example I need to explain that when I teach, I get excited about watching people's eyes light up with insight and understanding as they learn. I tend to be the poster girl for high positive energy.

In preparing for a class with this man, hearing '60s music in the background, I got up and started to dance to the fast tune. I suggested he join me, to boost our energy for the class. I'll never forget his response. He said, "I'll dance tomorrow."

I was struck by that because it suggested to me a postponement of a creative use of energy. That's not how I work. I think his response would make a great book title: *I'll Dance Tomorrow.* The book will talk about the peril of not living in the moment, of not using creative energy to live and work.

In a family, all family members may be in different states of energy at the same time and may prefer one state to another. A mother might have low, somewhat negative energy if she has been at home with the kids all day and barely survived many challenges. Her children might be pumped up for a sports practice, extracurricular class, or just the ability to go for a bike ride. Her husband might come home ready to interact and assume his part in parenting. Or he might need some time to reboot from a difficult day. If both people work, there are more varieties of energy that each parent will bring home. Homeschooling has its own stresses and the writings of Jamie C. Martin in *Steady Days* and her online blogs can be valuable resources. [2]

It doesn't matter who is in what state. What matters is that each member of the family be tuned in to one another and be sensitive to all states of energy that are swirling at one time.

The peril is that if one person is excited and pleased with an accomplishment, and another is upset because they are not having a good day, there could be a clash and a power struggle with one person thinking they are okay but the other person is not.

When my children were growing up, I could often be found singing to them, skipping, dancing, and otherwise sharing my energy as it bubbled up, from time to time. I can also be seen dancing with my husband in the kitchen, as I prepare dinner. When I surge with energy, I look for positive, creative, fun outlets for my surges.

I can also be low-key and still acknowledge the joy and positive energy that someone else is experiencing. I can do that because it is important to me to not be an obstacle for someone else. I can choose to say the words that show understanding. I can choose to simply be present to share an important moment. And when I choose not to, I can make it clear that it's because of my need for quiet, or solitude, or a timeout, and not because the other person isn't worthy.

The peril of not sharing your energy with others is that you might stifle the power surge and therefore miss an opportunity for sharing, intimacy, and fun. Don't do it.

CHAPTER 27

The Power of the Smile

Smiling is a beautiful thing.

I smile because I love to smile. It is a contagious facial expression. If you smile and can hold it long enough and are sincere, others smile back and something powerful is being exchanged without words. I also smile because I like other people and my smile is a gift of appreciation from me to them.

Smiling as a shared activity conveys acceptance and a little bit of joy. A smile lets the other person know that if they are not the sparkle in your eye, they have the potential to be.[1] Smiling says that the other person has just added value to your life because they are there, not because they have done something in particular.

The power of the smile is that it comes from the overflow of the heart and that deeply felt joy and pleasure in other people and the work they do is infectious. If you are someone who rarely consciously smiles because you think it may damage your credibility, pick a "Day to Smile," even if you think it'll kill you. You will find that **the smile has "gription"** and that's a powerful relationship tool.

Babysitting my youngest granddaughter, I am struck by the power of the smile. When she wakes up from a nap and I go into her room to lift her out of her crib, if I smile first, we begin to communicate non-verbally with smiles for a while, and we love the exchange. **Our smiles talk to each other.**

The lyrics of two classic songs about smiles highlight the power of the smile. The key phrases are "Light up your face with gladness" and "When you're smiling, keep on smilin', the whole world smiles with you."[2] When you smile, your entire demeanor changes. **A smile can not only change you, but it can change someone else, the person for whom your smile was intended.**

The manager I discussed in the section about "Facial Expressions" discovered that smiling had power. It seems that his mustache covered his laugh lines and so no one could tell whenever he smiled. He decided that the image others had of him was not who he was and he wanted to change people's perception of him, if he could. He was successful and **the lesson learned is that it IS possible to change the way others see us...if we want to.** This serious, imposing, very professional and successful manager decided to smile and sing and let others see it.

Smiling also affects vocal tone. There is a technique used in training customer service representatives who are phone counselors that teaches the rep to smile, even though the customers can't see him or her. Try it. Read something boring your normal way. What does it sound like? Now read the same thing with a smile on your face and notice how the vocal tone changes. You sound friendlier and more interesting.

When I was nineteen, at my mother's urging, I was a contestant in a beauty pageant. Not beautiful, I chose a song to show some talent so that people wouldn't notice my lack of prettiness. That song is still as important to me today as it was then: "Is It a Crime..." from *Bells Are Ringing.* [3]

"Is it a crime to start each day with a laugh, and a smile and a song?

And is it a crime to end each day with a laugh and a smile and a song?"

I smiled at nineteen and I still smile decades later.

Key Question to Consider:

Do you smile? Do you like to smile? How much smiling goes on where you work and in your home?

Potential Landmines of the Smile

A smile can be thought of sappy and sweet and insincere. Today's culture seems to value people, events and art that are edgy, not sweet and joyful.

To me those criticisms illustrate the peril of smiling in a world that loves "edge." Yet, for me, "If fifty thousand people believe a stupid thing, it is still a stupid thing." [4] I will not stop smiling.

CHAPTER 28

The Power of Connection

Some people "connect" with other people easily. They are so good at reading body language, decoding feelings, and "taking in that they form bonds and connect with others because that is their unique ability. This strength has the power of building strong relationships.

There is another kind of connection, that is, how we get from thought to thought. Very often, when we communicate, we don't take the time to break down our thoughts into small enough steps to enable others to see where we started, where we have ended up, and how we got there.

Two techniques to help others understand what you are saying are telling a story correctly and using powerful connection phrases.

The secret of telling a story so others will listen is to give the bottom line first and then follow up with details when invited to. This is the replacement for droning on while others are impatient for you to get the bottom line. Then, if they are interested, they can ask you leading questions or nod their heads as if to say, "Keep going. I want to hear more."

The second technique is one to use when you are trying to construct meaningful message points. Use this as a starter list, feel free to add to it, and it will help others follow what you are saying.

1. Lower than; higher than; less than; greater than
2. There's a discrepancy between _____ and _____.
3. Compared to _____
4. In contrast with _____, look at _____.
5. Look at the difference.
6. Look at the progression.
7. Look at the decline.
8. Look at the ascendance.
9. The significance of the relationship between _____ and _____ is _____.

10. This signals a change; this signals a big shift to the (left or right).
11. The past said _____; the present says _____; the future will say _____.
12. What you need to know is _____.
13. Implications for the future are:
14. It's clear that _____.
15. The puzzling thing is _____.
16. If you remember only one thing, _____.
17. The evidence shows _____.
18. Traditional perspectives show _____; controversial perspectives show _____.
19. I recommend _____without reservation.
20. I recommend _____ with reservation.
21. Truly remarkable; not significant
22. To review, _____.
23. This cemented the _____study once and for all.
24. This signifies a huge change.
25. The economic impact is _____.
26. The quality-of-life impact is _____.
27. The wild card is this: _____.
28. Here's the payoff: _____.
29. The fundamental flaw is _____; the remedy must include _____.
30. Despite the past, the future is…
31. These guidelines are the foundation of…

Key Question to Consider:

Do people have trouble following the logic of what you are saying? Do they have trouble understanding why you are telling them some information? Do they fail to grasp what you want them to do with the information?

If you have answered yes to any of these questions, use the phrases to guide others from thought to thought and see if they think you have become much easier to listen to.

More Questions to Consider

What information do I need to understand where my listener is coming from? Am I taking enough time with enough patience to connect? What do I need my listener to do or to say so that I will know that we have connected?

Prepare your answers before you begin sharing and you will connect and be heard.

Potential Landmines of No Connection

If you give people information and they don't know why, you will not be heard and you will not inspire follow-up action. It may seem ridiculous for you to go out of your way to connect the dots for others, but most of the time it is required.

Breaking information, ideas, and processes down into small steps and sharing them as you would a story, with a beginning, middle, and an end, is what people need. Begin communicating this way and wait until you notice that you have been heard. Then you can speed up.

But connect to where they are, that is, with little or no information, and then build from there.

No connection = no understanding = no buy-in and no action

CHAPTER 29
The Power of Etiquette and Tact

The first president of the US, George Washington, wrote "The Rules of Civility & Decent Behaviour in Company and Conversation" when he was fourteen and set forth one hundred and ten specific ways we should and should not behave, speak, or eat in public. [1] Even though every generation thinks they reinvent manners and codes of behavior for themselves, perhaps what is new is really very old. Read the entertaining book for yourself and see if you agree with me.

Communication etiquette rules may change; the need for excellent professional, family, and social talk never changes. Your success and use of appropriate language may seem invisible. Rudeness, uninformed behavior, selfishness, and lack of care as a communicator are very visible.

Look at GW's rule #35: "Let your discourse with men of business be short and comprehensive." Today I say, "Give the bottom line first and then use language with the skill of a surgeon." It's the same thing!

Rule #65 is violated daily. "Speak not injurious words, neither in jest or earnest; scoff at none although they give occasion." The plain language version might be, "Don't use your words to hurt others. Don't tease or use sarcasm, even though you think other people invite it." Yet how many places of work and homes use teasing, robust, or abusive language as the normal way people talk with each other? How many families think this kind of language is fun and "just the way we do things"?

Some people I have taught say they can't work without using banter, teasing, robust language, and verbal abuse—for example, in the New York metro area. (This might go as far north as New Hampshire and west into New Jersey and Pennsylvania.) They tell me, *"That's the way people talk and to buck that system would impair their ability to get work done and to motivate others."* That's also how they talk at home.

Some families that I have known can't have normal conversations without salty language, every day, every hour.

Almost every day, the media, politicians running for office, elected officials trying to hang onto their positions seem guilty of using reckless language and try earnestly to injure their opponents. They make fun of positions, sincerity, life styles and past behavior like it's an Olympic sport.

Nonetheless, that standard is not the way it ought to be. It just takes one or two courageous people to set a different standard and to be consistent in that effort. Call me a dreamer, but that's the way I see it. Bad habits can be changed. It takes a lot of effort, but it can be done. Two sisters, parents, cousins, or best friends in agreement can hold one another accountable for zero toleration of "bad" language. Then watch the law of multiplication take effect.

A word of caution is in order here. When you decide to buck a long-standing tradition of tolerating something that offends you and others in a business, other organization, or family, for example, lay the groundwork first. Over a period of a few weeks, first explain to others what you want to do and why it's important to you. Wait a few days for it to sink in and then repeat your goal.

Then poll the others to see if anyone else is on board. Wait for the timid to realize that this is an opportunity they may have been waiting for.

After a few more days, meet with at least one other person who has the same values and goals as you do. Devise a plan of action. What will you do, how you will do it, and what penalty will there be for non-compliance?

Then share this value, the goal, and the plan with everyone else. Make sure they understand it. Be clear, repeat yourself, and ask for a paraphrase.

Here's the rub. Be consistent; be utterly consistent. If you fail to comply once or twice, make a big deal about how you deviated, apologize, be up front about what was wrong, and what the consequences are for you and others. Then renew your efforts for zero tolerance.

It's remarkable how these efforts will begin to change the culture of your workplace, family, your community, or even government, one word at a time, one conversation at a time, and one relationship at a time. I have heard stories and talked to people who have been part of this culture change. It's real.

Another aspect of communication etiquette has to do with the problem of interruptions. The interruptions might be a phone call, a text message, or someone else bursting into your conversation, charging into your personal space uninvited.

Interruptions are about boundaries. Some people have no boundaries and think that they can interrupt any communication whether or not there is a verified emergency. Since no one can take advantage of you without your permission, the solution to inappropriate interruptions is for you to have ground rules about your boundaries and then to communicate them.

This was demonstrated clearly as I designed and taught a customer service program for a Vidal Sassoon hairstyling salon in Tysons Corner, Virginia. (This was before they were bought out by Regis.) The cornerstone of their workplace etiquette was that unless there is a life-threatening emergency, no one interrupts a stylist who is with a client. Zero tolerance. If a peer or boss needs to speak with a stylist who is with a client, they wait patiently in the background until they are recognized. Only then do they interrupt. When they do, they apologize to the client first, "Please excuse this interruption."

Translate this to your situation and you may have an opportunity to be a role model of etiquette.

Key Questions to Consider:

What would it be like if you gave your employees, peers, and boss complete focus when they needed you? What would it be like if when one of your children spoke to you, you gave them your full, undivided attention? What would it be like if when your spouse spoke to you, you did the same?

It is commonplace for parents to try to multitask and talk to kids, cook meals, do laundry, drive a carpool, and other necessary tasks all at the same time. And yet who has not had a child take your face in their hands and hold it still to get you to look at him or her and forget about other distractions?

When we don't give our children our undivided attention, we are giving them permission to do the same to us and to others. When we don't give our spouse our undivided attention, we are telling them that something or someone else is more important. In the workplace this holds true as well.

The Norman Rockwell painting of a husband and wife at the breakfast table with his newspaper as a boundary between them is a common joke. Cartoons mimic this, comedy routines refer to it, and the 2012 Oscar winner for best picture, *The Artist*, seems to have been inspired by the Rockwell pose.

When my husband is reading the newspaper, I know it's important to him. He loves to read the news in the paper form, rather than online. It is a highlight of his day. If I need to discuss something with him, or just need to be with him, I tell him, "I would like to talk with you about something. When is a good time?" That's a signal to him that I need more than an "uh-huh" and he respects me enough to tell me when he is ready. That doesn't mean he puts the paper down immediately. It just means that our communication process allows for one person to make a request for quality time. The other person tries to meet the need within a reasonable amount of time. And we both feel heard by the other person.

Friend Bart Tarman once talked to my husband and myself about the "etiquette of marriage." We had never thought about that before and, thinking strategically, we were taken by how this idea could transform a relationship, a family, a church, perhaps a nation. If people in relationships that lead to marriage knew and accepted the fact that there could be and should be etiquette to the marriage covenant, they might speak and behave with one another differently. We would be better examples to our children and our friends.

It's not acceptable marriage etiquette to call one another names, demean them publicly or privately, use violence in any way toward the other person, and to curse, spit, and yell. It shouldn't be acceptable business etiquette either, in my opinion.

How do you give attention to conversational etiquette with your co-workers, employees, family, and friends? Even if you don't see others being careful in this area, you can decide to do it anyway.

You can reprint this chart to have a regular checklist and assess how you are doing with etiquette and tact. I encourage you to make a copy to give to others. It will help you uncover blind spots.

Name of Person	Quality Time Today	Interruptions Today	Reflection, Apology Needed, Do-Over Required?
Co-worker			
Boss			
Peer			
Spouse			
Best friend			
Child #1			
Child #2			

Key Question to Consider:

Do you need new role models to exercise the power of etiquette and tact successfully?

Someone told me that the best role models are dead. He was referring to the fact that it may be easier to look at their whole lives for consistency and know that you probably won't find out some secrets that will jeopardize their examples in your eyes. In contrast, how many of us have had living role models that disappointed us?

List here the role models, dead or alive, whom I have admired:

Role Model	Key Characteristics	Ways You Are Like or Unlike
Aunt Fae— neighbor (not really a family member)	She was interested in me, loved me unconditionally, was an excellent homemaker, and always had time for a little girl who wanted to have tea with her.	She was satisfied to be a homemaker; my mom was not. She was a gifted baker; my mom was not. She was great at small talk; my mom was not. Actually, I am more like my mom in these areas, but I wanted to be like Aunt Fae.
Mrs. Rosemary Farley—high school English teacher	She had seemingly inexhaustible supplies of energy, was intelligent, and had passion for learning. She pursued under-achievers with the tenacity of a mother lion and hundreds of successful men and women thank her.	I almost match Mrs. Farley for energy and enthusiasm for teaching. I also have a passion to help others to achieve potential and unspoken dreams.

Lorraine Unger—best friend in high school	As a friend, she was loyal, patient, with a good sense of humor and patience with me.	She was patient and confident. I have not been. I am getting better. She reminds me of the woman cast in the role of the *First Lady's Detective Agency*, the British series about a clever African entrepreneur who set up her own business and became successful. She never succeeded at the expense of others' success. She was kind, patient, and very insightful.
Anne Boudiette— godmother	She was interested in everyone, cared about everyone, and seemed to love unconditionally. I always felt surrounded by her love and acceptance.	Working on it…
Now list yours:		

If you can't think of role models, either in your family or the world as a whole, I believe that many, many people have let you down and you are probably discouraged and depressed. Don't lose hope. You can still get reinvigorated by reading books, magazines, and newspapers to find someone you can look up to.

Start collecting stories for your "Role Model File." It will spur you on.

More Questions to Consider

Whom do you look up to? What compels you to find these people worthy of study, admiration, and respect?

For me I admire Nelson Mandela and other prisoners of war who survived imprisonment, Mother Theresa, the janitor who died and left over a million dollars to the school that employed him at twelve thousand dollars per year, and the hero of the kids book *Joseph Had a Little Overcoat* by Simms Taback. [2] In it, Joseph had a coat. Through many misadventures, he lost everything he had. **"So Joseph made a book about it. Which shows...you can always make something out of nothing."**

This quote shows that Joseph was content with a lot and also, with nothing, signs of integrity and contentment that I admire.

I collect stories about role models that I read about in newspapers, magazines, and books. William Kamkwamba of Malawi built a windmill to make electricity for his mom from a picture in a library book when he was fourteen. [3] He has inspired thousands of youth in Malawi to get an education and his success is raising money to pay for the education of others.

The Davert family is inspiring to me because, despite the challenges they have (cerebral palsy and brittle bone disease), they live life with enthusiasm, humor, and a real sense of adventure. [4] The story of Barry Hyde in the FAA is in the appendix: a pilot, who survived an accident, became blind, earned an MA and a PhD, and still works for the FAA. [5] Joni Erickson Tada is well known for her ministry of providing wheelchairs to handicapped people worldwide. A quadriplegic as a result of an accident when she was sixteen, she is married, an artist, and in full-time ministry.[6]

Going over this collection periodically refuels my resolve to do all that I can while I am able. I'd like to die at an old age, healthy, young at heart, and still giving to others.

Potential Landmines of Etiquette and Tact

If rudeness is the prized behavior in your work or family culture, you may have a lot of transforming to do. If you decide to take this on, you will be the odd person in the mix in need of support and encouragement. You need to make sure that you remain motivated and use role models to keep reinvigorating yourself when the going gets rough. Without a support group, you may not succeed.

CHAPTER 30

The Power of Encouragement

How many people feel as though they grew up in a military boot camp, without ever putting on a uniform or reporting for duty? I have no research to support this, but my impression is that more people suffer from bullying and verbal abuse than statistics show.

How would your friends, co-workers, and neighbors answer this question, "Do you think the best part of your life is ahead of you or behind you?" Their answers will give clues as to how secure and fearless they are and if they feel encouraged enough to think the way an entrepreneur thinks to make their own success.

Giving encouragement to others to dream and to translate those dreams into actions is a powerful gift. When we encourage others, we tell them we believe in them and their ability to grow and make a difference, to add value to their lives and to the lives of others.

Show me a person who does not live up to their potential and I will bet that person was bullied and verbally abused as a child by a parent, other family member, or significant person in that person's life.

My evidence comes from personal experience and observation.

Although I am an over-achiever and have had some great jobs and rewarding relationships since adulthood, nothing compares with the success I have achieved since I began to receive encouragement from people closest to me. I understand what it is to be loved, appreciated, and encouraged. My husband seems to be blind to my faults or he just doesn't care about them. Either way, I feel loved just because I exist.

When I am with my husband, I feel peace. The war zone of my developmental years is over. Consequently, I have been able to succeed in careers that I never even thought possible.

Every time you encourage someone else, you water their roots and give them an opportunity to grow into their full potential. When people are fending off constant criticism and negative feedback, they bend over to avoid being hurt by it. Trees that are continually buffeted by strong winds become crooked. So do people.

There is a true story of a woman whose jaw hurt her so much that after pursuing medical and spiritual options, the pain was still unbearable. Finally, after twenty-five years of marriage, she left her husband and her jaw stopped hurting. She must have been clenching her teeth so much that the pain never left the nerve endings around her jaw. Since that time, she has an even more impressive career.

How many prisoners of war have been able to survive the torture of their captivity and now thrive despite the former abuse? Nelson Mandela and John McCain come to mind and there are many others.

Key Questions to Consider:

How often do children need encouragement? As often as possible, on a daily basis
How often does a spouse need encouragement? DITTO
How often does a friend need encouragement? DITTO
How often does a co-worker need encouragement? DITTO
How often does an employee need encouragement? DITTO
How often does a boss need encouragement? DITTO
How often does a parent need encouragement? DITTO
How often does your pastor need encouragement? DITTO

Potential Landmines of Encouragement

I have been comparing people to plants and we know that some plants can be over-watered and some die or fail to thrive without enough water. Delicate orchids need water and putting a few ice cubes on top of their potting soil drips the right amount of moisture to the roots weekly. There is no one size fits all when we ask how much encouragement someone needs. It depends.

In a perfect world, we would all get as much encouragement as we needed. How do we know that measurement? Trial and error.

I prefer to err on the side of too much. The alternative is too painful to gamble with.

Encouraging people doesn't mean that you can't give constructive feedback or have boundaries. That's the key. When we encourage others, we must read their body language and listen for clues as to our effectiveness. We must care enough to tell others what could be done differently, not to tear them down but to build them up.

One thing that makes it hard to read the signs is insecurity. If the person we are trying to encourage is very insecure, they may not be able to receive encouragement at all. They may reject it, thinking, *That can't be for me. You are lying. I am not worth what you think I am. You'll find out, just as everyone else has.*

How do you tame an abused dog? One encouraging moment at a time. The same holds true for people. You can encourage them back to health, one bit of encouragement at a time.

If we want to encourage others successfully, we must be consistent and constant, persevering to the last day and our last breath. **If we lapse into selfish self-interest and stop encouraging others, we need to confess our lapse, ask for forgiveness, and renew our efforts. Who they become may depend on it.**

CHAPTER 31

The Power of Emotion

When I was going through a bad time, I had a conversation with a mentor. He simply asked me how things were going, the latest development in the saga of my turmoil. I told him a few things and he said nothing. He just stood there and a few tears rolled down his cheeks. I will never forget his compassion, which transcended any words he might have said. He said nothing. He just wept with me.

If we are able to share our feelings with others, we give them permission to do the same.

In a documentary of her methods, Winifred Ward, who taught creative dramatics for children, used a simple phrase. She would quietly talk to children who were acting out a fairy tale, for example, and say, "Are you sincere?" In her humble and unassuming way she helped release the power of emotion in the children actors.

I have thought about that phrase so many times as an adult. "Am I sincere? If not, what is getting in the way?"

There is a long story about why it has taken me so long to be sincere about my feelings, both to myself and to others. It involves parents who wanted me to be a certain way. Eager to please them, I lied to myself and pretended to feel what they wanted me to feel, think what they wanted me to think, and behave the ways they wanted me to behave. As an adult, I snapped to my senses and it has taken me years to unravel the damage done.

That's why I love the *Anne of Green Gables* series of books by Lucy Montgomery. In them, Anne seems to have a natural ability to tell the truth. It doesn't hurt her. In fact, she confesses to misbehavior she actually didn't commit, just to have another opportunity to confess. She got very good at it.

Mark Twain put it another way. He said, "If you tell the truth, you don't need such a good memory."

When we acknowledge our feelings, we can understand what makes us tick and then we can help others do the same. Check back to the long table of emotions I have included in this book to help you decipher yours.

Potential Landmines of Emotion

I remember an acting class I attended when I was about twenty-one. There was a young woman, a classmate who was filled with emotion, but she was afraid to express it. Actually, she was afraid if she released the emotion, the floodgates would open and not shut. She was afraid that there was too much unspent emotion inside of her and she was unequipped to let it out.

My acting teacher, Olympia Dukakis, used an acting exercise where this actress was encouraged to expose her feelings on a particular topic. I remember her yelling, crying, and pounding the floor with her fists. This went on for more than an hour. It is customary for actors to endure this type of exercise in order to understand who we are and how we can use ourselves as actors.

There was enough drama there for a few Greek tragedies. However, when Olympia asked her, after an hour, if she was done, she said, "No!" with energy, and so Olympia let the exercise go on for much longer.

It wasn't until well after two hours that this actress began to stop crying and look at this experience with some understanding. She had been afraid of letting all this emotion out, thinking it was "crazy" and that she would lose control of herself and "go crazy."

In fact, the opposite was true. She let out years of pent-up feelings in a safe environment, and when she was done, she was done. She was so relieved and she began to laugh, and we all laughed with her.

That's the peril of not dealing with feelings. They become so bottled-up that we become more afraid of the backlog than we have been of the original feelings, and we struggle to control the flood that will eventually break through.

Feelings have been put into us for a reason. They are part of the human experience. To ignore them, to disguise them, and to inhibit them will cause us harm in the long run.

When many people who give public testimonies (the tale of pain and redemption in their lives) cry, they tap into their joy of the story and the wave of emotion floods in. The person stands there and breathes and waits until they can climb on top of the wave, and then continues. Each time I watch this happen to someone else, it gives me permission to be more accepting of my own feelings. I am encouraged that our world is becoming more accommodating to people who share their feelings with others.

My third son cries when he is hurt, physically and emotionally. He told me when he was around eighteen, "Mom, I cry. I'm a real man and I cry. Don't worry. I'm okay. It's just who I am, a man who cries."

Another peril of holding back emotion is that it may be a symptom of the lack of self-knowledge. This can impair our ability to achieve intimacy with others and that is a peril indeed.

CHAPTER 32

The Power of Being Real

The power of being real includes being able to acknowledge, feel, understand, and share the present moment and emotion with others. It goes further.

When talking with someone, have you ever been asked, "Are you for real?"

To set context for some of my unusual ideas, I tell whomever I'm talking with that what they are about to hear is not fake or insincere but real. I tend to be optimistic and many people are not prepared to accept an optimistic viewpoint as relevant and worthy of consideration. It seems to me that if ideas don't have "edge" or attitude, they are often dismissed as irrelevant.

Happy, productive, healthy people with an optimistic outlook about life, are often regarded as weird or dismissed as out of touch. But that profile, happy and optimistic, is my normal, my "real."

So I sometimes preface my ideas with the opener, "I often hallucinate and here's a hallucination for you." I even go further, sometimes, to prepare others for my ideas. "I have been called many things in my life, but 'normal' and 'boring' are usually not what I am called."

I blame the media a lot for this dilemma. TV, film, and theater audiences have gotten used to, and seem to crave, more "yuck" than ever. I left the theater as a full-time career when I realized it focused primarily on the five D's: depression, despair, death, the devil, and disgusting details. This is not only the truth but it gets a big laugh. While laughing, people begin to think about their own TV, movie, and theater habits.

News programs on TV and radio compound this as many have become "info-tainment," not the voice of authority.

If people are happy, they are often dismissed as not being real.

Key Questions to Consider:

What is your "real"? Do you know? Are you satisfied with it? Have you ever changed from being less real to yourself and others to being more real?

We cannot have transparency in relationships, families, neighborhoods, communities and government unless we can be transparent and real to ourselves. The perspectives in this book, learning how to listen and how to speak more effectively, will help us be more real.

There may be a gap between how we see ourselves and how others see us. As hard as we can try to close the gap, it is impossible for us to have complete self-knowledge.

We can't. Body language experts, lie detectors, behavior detection specialists, private detectives all try to do it. But there is not any bit of science or human insight that is 100 percent correct.

In fact, when I get positive feedback, I'm not sure who people are talking about. I don't "get" me half the time. I've stopped worrying about it.

Potential Landmines of Being Real

There are perils of not being real, of being fake to oneself and to others. Relationships will be crippled and you will not be able to do your best for others or for yourself.

So which do you choose: death in life or death to a better life? I'm sorry to be so blunt, but I am just being real.

CHAPTER 33

The Power of How You Look

Although appearances are deceiving, and an incompetent manager or out-of-control person can dress to look competent and in control, the basic rule of thumb has not changed. "Clothes can make the person."

If you are a manager and you dress in a sloppy, unprofessional way, people, being visual, will create an identity for you in their minds that will not be flattering. On the other hand, if you consistently dress in a professional, tasteful manner, you will be thought of as worthy of respect, in charge, consistent, and trustworthy.

Likewise, if you are a parent and you show up at a parent teacher-conference in torn clothing that is wrinkled and stained, you will make a poor impression. If you show up from work in your suit or other professional attire, the teacher will have a more favorable opinion of you.

Many people say this is unfair. The unkempt-looking person may have just finished making an emergency tire change on the highway and had no time to clean up before the conference. And the professional person may be incompetent at what they do at work and are hanging on to their job by a thread, an expensive thread at that.

Communicating the gap between one's appearance and the wrong impression helps a lot. If I show up somewhere looking scruffy and I am expected to look sharp, if I mention it and give a brief explanation, I can manage the impression I create and help to make a better one.

Another factor that affects the power of how you look is that, in my opinion, it seems that many people have come to believe the way they dress is an entitlement. Some people believe that dressing the way they want to is their right, an avenue of self-expression that should not be curtailed or given boundaries in any way. The thinking goes like this: *How dare anyone tell me that I have to wear ironed khakis on casual dress days, or a collared shirt? How dare anyone tell me that my legs need to be covered with panty hose or tights when I wear a skirt or dress? How dare anyone tell me that my tattoos look unprofessional and should not be exposed to customers? How dare anyone tell me that I shouldn't wear earrings (man)? How dare anyone tell me that cleavage is out of place in the workplace, the grocery store, the mall, or anywhere except the bedroom?*

The list can go on and on.

Basically, the person in charge of your home, your office, your social group, your church or synagogue sets the gold standard. If the president of the US wears ties and jackets, then most men in business and government will want to do the same. When we have a female president, the same will hold true. If she were to wear suits, hose, sensible shoes, or fashion-forward shoes, whatever her professional attire will be, most women in authority will follow the trend. The same holds true for the spouse of the president.

When I teach, consult, or do any work where I am face-to-face with other professionals or customers, I dress in a skirt or pants suit, 100 percent of the time. I have been told that I look and act like a "solid professional," and I am sure that my appearance deserves some of the credit. I like to look this way. It enhances my confidence and credibility in my own eyes as well as the eyes of others.

A woman asked me to mentor her in the area of her professional image. She wanted me to critique her attire, her hair, and the way she spoke. I tested her resolved to want to change and I thought she was sincere. After I pointed out the gaps between her professional desires and her actual practices, it became clear that she was not open to change. I backed off and the last time she asked for my help, I said, "Please don't ask me. I don't think you are really interested in changing."

Excerpted from my book *Strategies for Fashion in the Workplace* is this advice:

> But this rule remains. Your credibility in the workplace is greatly influenced by what you wear and don't wear. I have always dressed for the job I wanted to have: top-of-the-line consultant with a six-figure income. I want to look the part. And it has always paid off. [1]

Add to this what I believe: **your credibility in the marketplace of the world and even the sanctity of your home is also greatly influenced by what you wear and don't wear.**

Potential Landmines of How You Look

When I was twenty-three with a full-time teaching job at Queens College in NYC, I enjoyed sitting in the back of the room incognito for the first ten minutes on the first day of class. With long hair to the middle of my back and a trendy tent dress with knee-high boots, I looked like one of the students. In fact, we were almost the same age.

When the students had waited the obligatory ten minutes for the professor to show up and then began to gather their things to leave, I would stand up and move to the front of the room as I introduced myself. Since I looked like them, I had to use other means to be the teacher and in charge. I told them my name was "Miss Kamp" and I quickly handed out my syllabus and went over the rules and classroom guidelines.

If I had not done that, the gap between how I looked and my positional authority in the class (the boss) would have been non-existent. I lived the peril that year because I was not comfortable dressing one level up. The insecurity in asserting one's position is so common for young teachers and perhaps my experience here will encourage other people to avoid this trap.

I'm not saying that young people need to look ridiculously old to be accepted as a boss or parent or teacher or lawyer or judge. I am saying that if you don't look the part, if you are very young, you can use some common sense to try and dress the part. It helps others see you in the role you are playing.

I have seen parents go to parent teacher conferences or school plays dressed like their kids. Children want their parents to be parents and dressing the part helps.

There is a play, *The Importance of Being Earnest,* where an orphaned girl, finally discovers who she is by the way people look at her, in the last act. If people look at us and don't see what they expect, it may impact our effectiveness in ways we don't intend. Just sayin'.

Typically, I cling to the old-fashioned rule of thumb: a facilitator or a manager, an executive, and a parent should dress the part. That means you should wear clothing that says, "There is at least one level of experience and authority between us." It also means that you know things and have some experience, wisdom, discernment, and qualifications that distinguish you from those you serve. I think that this makes it easier for others to relate to you. After all, it's not about you, it's about them.

CHAPTER 34

The Power of Expectation, Curiosity, and Wonder

Key Question to Consider:

What would you be like if you woke up every day in a state of wonder?
- I wonder what my employees or children or best friend will discover today.
- I wonder who will make me laugh today.
- I wonder if I will make anyone else laugh today.
- I wonder what I will learn today.
- I wonder what I will learn today.
- I wonder who I will love today.
- I wonder who will love me today.
- I wonder what questions I will ask that will open doors for at least one other person.
- I wonder who will ask me a question that will challenge and improve me.
- I wonder how my family will meet or exceed my expectations of them.
- I wonder how I will exceed their expectations of me.
- I wonder how I will exceed my own expectations of me today.

Potential Landmines of Expectation and Wonder

I am convinced that if we don't have a sense of wonder and expectation in the way we live, we are in jeopardy of becoming the dead walking. Without curiosity and expectation, we are zombies taking up space but not improving or enriching it.

There are no perils of living in expectation, curiosity, and wonder. Guaranteed.

CHAPTER 35

Where Do You Go from Here?

Whether I have been teaching acting for the theater or communication skills for managers, lawyers, scientists, parents, and friends, I have always issued an invitation for average to become above average and for excellence to become brilliance.

How does that work? If you want to be successful and love your life, the choice is yours. **Where is it written that you can't reinvent your life for yourself and for those you live with?**

It is up to you to reinvent your leadership for yourself and for others. You may have had role models who inspired you or role models who turned you off. Now is the opportunity for you to reinvent what you do and how you do it.

Others call this customizing your work, making it your own, and knowing that "one size doesn't not fit all." I call it **reinvention**. When you redefine what you do and how you do it, through the blood, sweat, and tears of your own experience, you are using your unique ability. Remember the "Circles of Abilities" earlier in this book? The inner circle is your ability to recognize your unique ability and to use it in your life. When you do, you will inspire others to do the same.

Successful people don't reinvent themselves because of what others will say. They are glad they "get to." They do it because of how gratifying it will be to live well and leave their mark in life for the future.

Footnotes

Chapter 1—The Power of Perspectives

1. *Jane Austen and the Canterbury Tale* by Stephanie Barron, p. 17
2. From an article in *The New Yorker* magazine, January 30, 2012

Chapter 2—The Power of Caring

1. Friesen, James, Ph.D., E. James Wilder, PhD., Anne M. Bierling, M.A., Rick Koepcke, M.A., and Maribeth Poole, M.A., *Living from the Heart Jesus Gave You*, Pasadena, Shepherd's House, Inc., 1999

Chapter 6—The Power of the Zip as Wait

1. Bill Smith of Motorola developed Six Sigma ® as a quality control system, "a set of practices designed to improve manufacturing, processes and eliminate defects," and later expanded it to other types of business processes. Six Sigma ® and Lean Six Sigma ®, like Lean Cuisine ®, mean less fat and more to the point.
2. *Strength Finders 2.0* by Tom Rath was developed by the Gallup Poll organization. You have to buy the book to get the barcode to go online to take the assessment, which measures your top five strengths out of a possible thirty-four. "Woo" refers to a person's ability to go into a group of strangers and connect with them in powerful ways. The person who excels in "woo" doesn't necessarily make these people friends for life. It's just a strength that can be used again and again without the wooer feeling the need to follow up later with the people who have been wooed.

3. One of one hundred and ten rules in George Washington's *Rules of Civility & Decent Behaviour in Company and Conversation*, which he wrote at age fourteen.

4. Father Powell's books are: *The Secret of Staying in Love*, *Why Am I Afraid to Tell You Who I Am?* and *Will the Real Me Please Stand Up?* published by Argus Communications, a division of DLM Inc., Niles, Illinois, 60648; they are out of print.

5. I've spoken to someone who used to work for Argus Communications, now defunct, and he said that I could reprint with their permission. Please note I have tweaked the original list for clarity.

Chapter 9—The Power of the Question

1. Plans to publish *The Actor's Working Process* are underway. If you are interested in a copy, contact me at: askjill@strategiesforlivingun limited.com.

2. Malcom Gladwell, author of *Outliers: The Story of Success* (NY: Little, Brown, and Company, 2008), describes the method a math teacher used to teach a young adult math. He coached her by asking questions and videotaped the process: "Twenty-two minutes pass from the moment Renee begins…to the moment she says, 'Ahhhh,'" p. 245. He suggests that if the teacher interfered with the process, the student might never have learned the math, even though her desire to learn was great: "Success is a function of persistence and doggedness and the willingness to work hard for twenty-two minutes to make sense of something that most people would give up on after thirty seconds," p. 246
I am extending that insight to suggest that interrupting thinking after powerful questions are asked can cripple learners.

Chapter 11—The Power of Arresting, Compelling Language

1. Dick, a member of the pastoral teaching team at Timberline Church in Fort Collins, Colorado, helps to mentor the pastoral staff and works throughout the city with the larger leadership community. Through the years, the themes of relationship-building and reconciliation have become central to Dick's speaking and writing. Invitations to speak on

those topics have taken Dick across many denominations and cultures. His background includes a pastorate in Illinois (1966–1978), president of Bethany College, California (1978–1992), and in the spring of 1993, he served as minister-in-residence at Gordon-Conwell Seminary, South Hamilton, Massachusetts. The Foths moved to Washington, DC, in August of 1993 to work in man-to-man disciplining and the Prayer Breakfast Movement, nationally and internationally. That's where I met him, in 2002, when I helped out.

2. I even bought the domain name: www.stickygription.com.

Chapter 12—The Power of Truth

1. This quote is by Anatole France a French novelist from the 19th Century.

Chapter 14—The Power of Setting Context

1. Patterson, Kerry, Joseph Grenny, Ron McMillan, Al Switzler, *Crucial Confrontations*, NY: McGraw Hill, 2005
2. This premise is the heart of the book *Crucial Confrontations*.
3. Patterson, Kerry, Joseph Grenny, Ron McMillan, Al Switzler, Crucial Conversations, updated second edition, NY: McGraw Hill, 2012

Chapter 16—The Power of Eye Contact

Footnotes for research on infants and eye contact:
1. Samuels, CA "Attention to eye contact opportunity and facial motion by three-month-old infants," *J Exp Child Psychology* (August 1985),
2. Hains, SM, Muir, DW "Infant sensitivity to adult eye direction," *Child Dev* (October 1996),
3. Farroni, T, Johnson, MH, Csibra, G (October 2004), "Mechanisms of eye gaze perception during infancy," *J Cogn Neurosci* 16 (8): 1320–6
4. Reid, VM, Striano, T (March 2005), "Adult gaze influences infant attention and object processing: implications for cognitive neuroscience," *Eur J Neurosci*

5. Brooks, R, Meltzoff, AN "The importance of eyes: how infants interpret adult looking behavior." *Developmental Psychology* (November 2002)

Chapter 17—The Power of "Taking In"

1. Subtext is the words beneath the words, the thoughts, feelings, and questions that are implied in dialogue but not spelled out by a playwright.
2. Friesen, James G., PhD, and others. *Living from the Heart Jesus Gave You*, Pasadena: Shepherd's House, Inc., 2000, website: www.lifemodel.org/index.php

Chapter 18—The Power of Patience

1. My first son had wisdom about this even when he was a teenager. I have never forgotten what he said. In fact, he will laugh as he reads this chapter because he reminds me about my need to develop patience, something I am short of.

Chapter 19—The Power of Discernment

1. For more about Murray Kilgour, check out: http://www.transformconsulting.net; for Dan Sullivan: www.strategiccoach.com; Nomura, Catherine and Julia Waller, *Unique Ability: Creating the Life You Want*, Toronto: The Strategic Coach, Inc., 1995
2. The first version of this assessment was in *Now, Discover Your Strengths* by Marcus Buckingham and Donald O. Clifton. The second version is similar, *Strength Finders 2.0*. As of this writing there are two others to consider, *Strength Based Leadership* by Tom Rath and Barry Conchie, and *Standout* by Marcus Buckingham. These are all products of the Gallup Poll organization.

Chapter 21—The Power of Vocal Tone

1. Available in paperback. I have the original hardcover from the first printing in in 1976, Drama Book Specialists.

2. Most professional theater companies in large cities have at least one actor who is trained in the Linklater approach and perhaps they can coach you.
3. To learn more about the Alexander Technique, check your library or local book store. There are hundreds of books published. A professional theater may also know of an Alexander Technique teacher in your area.
4. From the *Wall Street Journal*, April 28, 2011
5. Published February 2012, Dow Jones & Company, Inc.

Chapter 23—The Power of Articulation

1. The uvula is the skin that hangs down in the back of your throat. If you look in a mirror and open your mouth wide, and if you can relax the back of the tongue so you can see, you will see the uvula. It is attached to the soft palate, the muscle that raises and lowers in the back of your mouth when you speak. Any basic speech book has a picture of this.
2. This story was told in the 1960s in the acting classes I attended at the Herbert Bergdorf Studio and The American Academy of Dramatic Arts in New York City.

Chapter 25—The Power of Facial Expressions

1. This is from "My Girl," made famous by the Temptations.
2. In the theater, it is common for a director of musicals to bark instructions at the actors while they are rehearsing on stage. If a director yells out, "Teeth!" to the actors, what the director wants is for the actor to smile so the audience can see teeth. This makes the actors look happy and inspires the audience to be happy, too.

Chapter 26—The Power of Energy

1. Jim Loehr and Tony Schwartz have written a book that is practical and insightful to help people change the way they manage their energy, NYC, Free Press, 2003.

2. Martin, Jamie C., Steady Days: A Journey Toward Intentional, Professional Motherhood, NYC: Infused Communications, 2009; Mindset for Moms: From Mundane to Marvelous Thinking in Just 30 Days, a Kindle Book, 2012

Chapter 27—The Power of the Smile

1. Friesen, James G., PhD, and others. Living from the Heart Jesus Gave You, Pasadena: Shepherd's House, Inc., 2000, website: www.lifemodel.org/index.php
2. The first song's lyrics were written by John Turner and Geoffrey Parsons, music by Charlie Chaplin, and made famous by Judy Garland, Nat King Cole, and Jerry Lewis. Second song by Louis Armstrong.
3. This musical comedy was written by Betty Comden and Adolph Green and the music was composed by Jule Styne. Invite me to teach for you and invariably I will sing it.
4. I am repeating this quote because I use it so often.

Chapter 29—The Power of Etiquette and Tact

1. Published by Applewood Books in 1998, this book is available from Amazon Books and from many government gift shops in Washington, DC.
2. Penguin Putnam Books, NYC, 1999
3. http://williamkamkwamba.com
4. http://devertfamilyblogs.blogspot.com and Michigandifference.org
5. "Clear skies ahead: Job with FAA latest comeback step since losing sight in plane crash," Kathy Chaffin, Published Friday, December 25, 2009, 2:00 AM
   ANNAPOLIS—It has been almost nine years since the Post ran a story about Barry Hulon Hyde's brush with death in a plane crash.
   It was a story of miraculous survival, the unwavering love of a family and tremendous faith.
   Hyde, who lost his eyesight in the crash, was quoted in the Nov. 12, 2000, story as saying, "The good Lord's got a purpose for me..."
   He was right.

To recap what happened:

June 1, 1998: Twenty-six-year-old Barry Hyde was flying high—literally. A 1990 graduate of South Rowan High School, he had completed flight school at American Flyers in Addison, Texas, in January 1996 and was enjoying his job as an instructor for Lancaster Aviation at Concord Regional Airport.

Hyde had completed a morning flight and was flying to Roanoke, Va., in a Piper Twin Comanche as safety pilot for another pilot who was working on getting his instrument ratings current. Thirty minutes into the flight, the right engine failed, then the left.

Hyde's left eye was ripped out on impact, and the damage to his right eye was severe. Doctors said the bones in his face were crushed, describing it as an "eggshell crushed in 10 million pieces," according to his mother, Brenda.

Surgeons grafted tissue and bone and used 15 steel plates to rebuild his face.

February 1999: For the first time, Hyde was alert enough to become fully aware of what had happened. He wanted to die and talked openly about suicide.

His steady girlfriend, having stuck by him while he was in the hospital and rehabilitation center, had broken up with him months before, saying "she couldn't handle it anymore."

July 1999: Hyde underwent another surgery at Carolinas Medical Center in Charlotte, during which a plate was put in to lift his nose from his face and several screws from the previous surgery were removed.

August 1999: He enrolled at the N.C. School for the Blind, living on campus while learning to get around, read Braille and work on the computer using software designed for the blind.

Dec. 30, 1999: Hyde's father, Barry Edward Hyde, died suddenly at age 55 after four surgeries following a massive heart attack.

April 2000: Hyde interviewed as a candidate for the Southeastern Guide Dog School program in Palmetto, Fla.

June 6, 2000: He took an aviation test and became the first and only blind advanced ground instructor.

June 12, 2000: Hyde was matched with a 19-month-old, black Labrador retriever named Lincoln.

The dog became his constant companion, helping to heal him emotionally and regain his freedom.

October 2000: He earned his aviation license to become an instrument ground instructor.

About a month after the story ran, Hyde met Kendra, a blind woman who was taking classes at the University of North Carolina at Charlotte, and they began dating.

In May of 2001, Hyde was accepted at UNC-Charlotte, and he and Lincoln moved to a nearby apartment. "We walked back and forth to class," he says, "1,800 steps one way."

Life as a blind student was challenging, but Hyde recorded the lectures on a tape recorder and played them back at home, using another tape recorder to make verbal notes.

He took his tests at the university's Disability Services Office on a computer with JAWS (Job Access With Speech) software, allowing him to take them verbally.

The N.C. Division of Blind Services paid Hyde's tuition and assisted with his expenses and rent.

He graduated in December of 2004 with a 3.45 grade-point average.

Lincoln led him across the stage to accept his diploma at commencement services, and the audience honored them with a standing ovation.

"It was really awesome to be recognized like that," Hyde says.

The following May, he underwent another surgery on his face, during which surgeons removed several metal plates and screws and took bone from his cranium to rebuild his face and nose.

In July 2005, Hyde moved to Daytona Beach, Fla., and began working on his master's degree in aeronautics at Embry-Riddle Aeronautical University, the world's largest flight school.

He received financial assistance from the Florida Services for the Blind, a $12,000 scholarship from the university and several other scholarships, including two from the Greater Miami Aviation Association's Batchelor Aviation Scholarship Fund and two from the Air Traffic Control Association.

He had only been there four months when Kendra died suddenly from complications of diabetes. "It was a heartbreaker," he says. "Lincoln and I came home for her funeral service."

When Hyde returned home to Annapolis a month later for the holidays, he and his cousin took Kendra's ashes up in an airplane, releasing them over both their homes.

The following year, Hyde's friendship with Nancy Riedel developed into a romance. They had gotten to know each other when he spoke at fundraisers for the Carolina Outreach Program of Southeastern Guide Dog Inc., of which she was director.

When the Concord outreach program closed a few months later, she and her Labrador retriever, Jackson, a retired guide dog, moved to Daytona Beach to be with Hyde and Lincoln. Soon afterward, Riedel, who Hyde calls "Nance," got a job with Embry-Riddle.

Hyde remained dedicated to his studies, graduating on May 7, 2007, with a 4.0 grade-point average with distinction.

"I had lots of family and friends there for the commencement," he says. "Lincoln was hooded when I got hooded."

And when Hyde and Lincoln walked across the stage at commencement services, they received another standing ovation. "I was the first blind graduate in Embry-Riddle's 84-year history," he says. On June 1 of that year, Hyde began working on his doctorate online from Northcentral University in Prescott, Ariz.

"It was almost like it was God's plan that I started on the nine-year anniversary of the plane crash," he says. "That was the driving force for me to prove that I could continue on."

Hyde received two more scholarships from the Greater Miami Aviation Association and Air Traffic Control Association. He has received 25 scholarships in all, continuing work on his doctorate with a 2011 completion date for his dissertation.

Last Dec. 3, Hyde's faithful guide dog, Lincoln, was retired to the status of beloved pet. On Jan. 20 of this year, Jet, another black Lab, took over as his guide dog.

"Jet is a city dog," he says. "He grew up in Albany, N.Y."

Hyde says there's never a dull moment for him and Riedel with their three dogs, each one valued at $60,000.

While continuing to work on his doctorate this spring, Hyde taught an online aviation class for Daniel Webster College in New Hampshire. The topic of his dissertation: "The Proper Execution of the Preflight Checklist to Ensure Flight Safety."

Hyde says the pilot's failure to properly execute the preflight checklist was the cause of his June 1, 1998, crash. He is working on a book about the crash and his struggle to remain in aviation as a blind man.

It will be titled, *Seeing New Horizons: How Blind Aviator Barry Hulon Hyde Views Aviation Safety.*

In early October, Hyde flew with Riedel, Lincoln and Jet to Washington, D.C., where he received his fourth scholarship from the Air Traffic Control Association on Oct. 7. The next day, Hyde interviewed for an aviation safety analyst position with the Federal Aviation Administration (FAA).

The interview was held on the eighth floor of the FAA's Flight Standards District Office in downtown Washington, he says, and lasted two hours. Later that afternoon, the deputy director of communications for the FAA did a live interview with Hyde and Jet for its Web site.

The next day, Hyde met FAA Administrator Randy Babbitt at a Combined Federal Campaign Kickoff that encouraged employees to donate money to nonprofits. Speaking in front of an audience of more than 150, Hyde told them about his plane crash and how he had benefited from various nonprofit organizations for the blind.

As part of the event, Hyde presented Babbitt with an alumni pin from Embry-Riddle, his alma mater, and Babbitt returned the favor with a limited edition book on the history of the FAA.

Hyde, who contacted the *Post* when he arrived in Annapolis last week to spend Christmas with his mother, says he was offered the job on Dec. 3— Lincoln's 11th birthday. "Once again, I think that's God's way of showing how He's continuing to make things very memorable for me," he says.

Part of his duties when he begins work on March 1 will be developing policies and procedures for general aviation and flight school.

"This is just a huge honor," Hyde says. "This is what I've worked so hard for for the past 10 years. It's like a dream come true.

"It shows me that God has a purpose for me and that He's making it known with each door that opens up."

6. See Joni's website: www.joniandfriends.org. Read her biography, *Joni Erickson Tada: Her Story*, 1998. She also has written many other books of encouragement and wisdom.

Chapter 33—The Power of How You Look

1. My book will be available soon as an e-book. Look on my website for the announcement: www.strategiesforlivingunlimited.com.

Made in the USA
Lexington, KY
26 May 2013